FROM
THUNDER TO SUNRISE

Reflections of Vietnam
by Corbin Lee Cherry

TURNER PUBLISHING COMPANY

Turner Publishing Company

Library of Congress Catalog Card Number: 95-60328

ISBN: 978-1-56311-179-2

Additional copies may be purchased directly from the publisher.

FROM THUNDER TO SUNRISE
REFLECTIONS OF VIETNAM

These pages, these feelings, these memories,
these thoughts and these words are dedicated
to the men and women who served this country
in the war known to all of us who were there
as Vietnam. A bond will forever join us
together because of that place, that time
and those memories.

PRELUDE

The following pages are the result of a great many men
and women who spent a part of their life in
the southeastern corner of Asia, in a small country called
Vietnam. That time was to change their lives in a varied
number of ways. The change was to affect them, most of
them, for the rest of their lives.

My hope in writing these words and filling these pages
is that someone who was there might come to know that
there are many others who also feel as they do, be that
good or bad. The truth to this whole story and the fulness
of this story may never be told, but I would hope that this
could be a part of the puzzle. In writing this I learned
a lot about what happened to me there and later here.

The time for healing is past due. The time for us to band
together in hope is right now. The time for love to be
felt, by giving and receiving, is right now. We were in
that thing together and we are in this thing of healing
together. The time is at hand.

We shall never forget that place and that time. That
would be to rob us of a time when many young people lost
their innocence, but we can live with the fact that we
were there and we have survived to this point; many of
our band never did get this far, for a thousand different
reasons.

The time is at hand to reach out and take each other's
hand, for we are all brothers and sisters from that war and that time.
Reach out, touch someone who was there and tell them
that you love them and you are glad that they got home.
Welcome back ..... Here the healing starts ....

TABLE OF CONTENTS

PART ONE
GETTING TO "IT"

PART TWO
"IT"

PART THREE
GETTING AWAY FROM "IT"

ABOUT THE AUTHOR: CORBIN LEE CHERRY
Minister, Composer, Lecturer, Author, Sportman, Musician, Patriot

MILITARY SERVICE

U.S. Army, June, 1967-April, 1974
Received medical retirement as Captain due to wounds suffered in Vietnam.

1967-1968	Fort Bragg, 82nd Airbone Division
1968	Military Academy, West Point, New York
1969	Vietnam, 101st Airborne Division
1970	Walter Reed Medical Center, Washington, D.C.
1971-1974	Letterman Medical Center, San Francisco, California

Awards and Decorations:

5 Air Medals, 1 Army Commendation Medal,
3 Purple Hearts, 1 Vietnamese Cross of Gallantry,
1 Bronze Star, 2 Silver Stars

VARIOUS MINISTRIES

1962-1964	Bath, North Carolina
1964-1966	Goldsboro, North Carolina
1967-1974	Chaplain, U.S. Army
1974-1978	Parish Minister, Mill Valley, California
	Night Club and Street Ministry, San Francisco
	Ski Ministry with handicapped children, California
1978-1982	Chief of Chaplains for the Veterans Administration, Washington, D.C., this is the second largest Chaplain Service in the world
1982-Present	Chief, Chaplain Service, VAMC, San Francisco, California

PROFESSIONAL AFFILIATIONS

The North Carolina Conference of the United Methodist Church
The Northern California Conference of the United Methodist Church
The National Inconvenienced Sportsman's Association
The National Amputee Golf Association
The International Sportsman's Association
The Disabled American Veterans
The Military Order of the Purple Heart

LITERARY ENDEAVORS

Published in the area of the Vietnam Veteran, his stress and after war existance.
One song "L.A. Lady" has been recorded and sold.
Published in the area of the handicapped person and how they deal with their environment.
Published in the area of the burned patient and what chaplains role is in their life.
Written articles on the aging process, orthopedic patients, substance abuse and dying.
Published two books of poetry and prose.

Introduction

I'd like to introduce you to Corbin Cherry. He is a Minister, Composer, Musician, Author, Lecturer, Sportsman, and Patriot. I firmly believe he can be an asset to your organization, whether it is business, civic, religious, professional health care, a sports club, or veterans group. If this seems like a varied group of interests, it is- Corbin Cherry has been a part of each of these groups. He has been a part of many lives, one of which is mine. I believe you and your organization will receive inspiration and reap the benefits from this man's ability and life story.

Barry J. Speare
Executive Director
Summit Productions

A Ministry To Be Shared

Corbin Cherry is an ordained Methodist minister and is presently the Chief Chaplain at the VA Medical Center, San Francisco, California. From 1978 to 1982 Corbin Cherry served as the Chief of Chaplains for the Veterans Administration and was responsible for the spiritual care of veteran patients in 172 Veterans Administration Hospitals in the United States and Puerto Rico.

Prior to joining the VA in 1978, Corbin was a hospital chaplain, a parish minister, and a nightclub entertainer who developed a special ministry among the "night people." Corbin has taken his ministry from the quiet rural eastern coast of North Carolina to the jungles of Vietnam, and the streets of San Francisco, and back to the busy hub of our nation in Washington, D.C.

A Ministry of Variation

While serving as a chaplain in Vietnam, Corbin was attached to the 101st Airborne Division. While on a rescue mission, he stepped on a landmine and lost one of his legs. As he lay in his hospital bed, unsettled and crying at the sight of the Commanding General of the 101st at his bedside, he apologized for his tears. The General took his hand and looked at him saying, "You go ahead and cry, I have nothing more important to do than this." This bit of encouragement caused Corbin to adopt the same feeling in his life for others from that time on. This is seen in his understandable interest in the handicapped person. He has used his talents in a teaching ministry to handicapped people in several sports, notably snow skiing and golf. He is a certified ski instructor and a low handicap golfer who was featured in *Golf Digest* in 1981.

Outreach Ministry

As the author of music, poetry, and three books to be published, Corbin Cherry can bring a new fresh look to the ministry and the idea of caring. As a former orthopedic patient and amputee, he speaks with authority on the subject of ways to deal with the handicapped. He has published papers on the aged, substance abuse, and the terminally ill patient. As a very dedicated person to both God and his country, he brings a warm glow to the idea of being an American. He is a witty speech maker, a somber orator, and one who brings important issues to the point of truth. He is well-versed in both medical and nonmedical ethics and has lectured extensively on the subject. As a chaplain in Vietnam, he received the Silver Star, 3 Purple Hearts, the Bronze Star, 5 Air Medals, and the Vietnamese Cross of Gallantry.

QUOTES AND COMMENTARY

"Corbin Cherry inspires others with physical disabilities to go on competing in the bigger game of life." *Golf Digest*, February, 1981

"Chaplain Cherry, I count on your support in our efforts to make that new beginning we all desire." Ronald Reagan, President of the United States, February, 1981

"His music brings him satisfaction- that's what it comes down to." William Steif, *Washington Post*

"It was an honor and a privilege to welcome you as guest Chaplain in the House of Representatives' Chamber." Congressman G.V. (Sonny) Montgomery, Chairman, House Veterans Affairs Committee, October, 1981

"I admire your devotion and inspiring courage, and deeply appreciate the comfort you bring to your wounded comrades." General William C. Westmoreland, Chief of Staff, August, 1969

PART ONE
GETTING TO "IT"

A Different Play

The rising moon brings me memories
and it will soon shed a definite light
on a rather dark, unthoughtful world and time
and to those underneath it.

That tree line there against the sky
is almost obliterated in the near dark
and gives life to one's imagination of impressions
of thousands of empty arms reaching out.

The breathe of the wind
is ever so slight,
all is nearly still as if waiting
the coming source of nocturnal light and quiet.

The air is getting cooler
and the moment is at hand
when a flood of light
will surge on this stage for humanity.

So we must get on board
and face our trip to the reality
that will cause this evening
to sort of disappear from our memory base.

For tomorrow will indeed be different,
for I will stand then and observe
that all of these same characters
will provide a totally different play.

The air will be filled with noises,
as the voices of men and machine ring out
and time will cause this night to fly away
and we will be reminded of war ....

Getting To "It"

My mind is filled with all of the images
that make up the visions that I have just now,
as I race toward my time of war.

I do not know what is out there waiting,
I just know that it has to be something
that will change my life forever.

There is a sensation surging through my veins
like unto a pump that forces the blood
at a rate far faster than normal.

Maybe I have heard too many stories,
maybe I have read too many newspapers,
maybe I am just frightened by this whole voyage.

This trip seems to be taking forever
and I cannot sleep for my mind is cascading
like a giant waterfall after the spring thaw begins.

I wonder what my family is doing right now.
I know they must think of me as I do of them.
I pray they are safe as they enter slumber tonight.

I must try and sleep, for come the morning
I will be there in the midst of the heat
and in the midst of war, my first time.

I do not know how I will feel about seeing people die
or even seeing them weep from loss or fear
or knowing that either could be me.

My mind is still very busy as I try to sleep.
I can only imagine what is out there waiting.
All of these soldiers are drinking and laughing,

I hope they will laugh for a long, long time ....

I Would Like To Know

I would like to know that if the world stood still
would there be a place for me to rest my mind?
I would like to know if it started up again,
would I be captive or free?

I am sure that I would not be totally free
because I also know that in this sphere of time
there exist inside of my heart feelings
which my mind can only fear.

To be free one has to know
that someone someplace has a part,
in making him something different, special if you will,
instead of tearing to pieces his already fragile mind.

I would like to know that if time truly stopped
and tomorrow never really arrived
would I have the strength to even care
or even the desire to survive another day like today?

I know that I will feel
some sense of relief
with the passing of this long night's trek
and the coming of still another day.

To not be afraid in these days
one has to know for certain
that there exists a clear path
which can grant serenity at it's end.

I would like to know that if this life stopped
would I be ready for the end of time
or would I be just another limb
that has found no room to bend?

I know I will always be the one
who questions what is out there,
even though I know it is something that I cannot control,
no matter whether it be life or death.

I do know on the eve of this new chapter in my life
that if the world stopped and life ended for me,
that little things like death could not harm me,
for my soul will not perish.

So I enter this new time in my life
uninformed of many things,
unsure of many others,
but sure of what is important.

The Moon Is On The Wing

The time has come and the clock is running,
but still there is time to think
on what tomorrow will bring.

Leaving home to cross the world,
to see sights virgin to these eyes,
knowing that from here I will be banished for a time.

The moon is full tonight, her time to shine,
lighting a path for someone like me,
the moon is on the wing.

The cities down below sparkle in the night,
but out there the fog sits like a visible spirit,
waiting for time to allow it to enter.

A vast stream of light the moon gives off tonight
and as I sit and watch from this window
it mobilizes my emotions.

The stars all seem to be stationary as we pass through the night,
yet not many can be seen
for the moon is on the wing.

Clouds can be seen now as over them we pass
and as these eyes view them
there is an urgent need to cry.

The moon holds a special peace for me
when I see those rays of light,
emotions indeed seek release.

The moon is on the wing and tonight that is special
for it has given me peace,
I am glad it is not raining.

Surely when people see this sight there is a thrill,
not because of where they are going,
but because the moon is on the wing.

The world, in my mind seems so soft and peaceful,
makes one almost forget as I sit up here,
that out there somewhere the war is waiting.

Little Cloud

Overhead the stars do shine brightly,
they are the same as they are back home,
but in the midst of the mass of stars
there is a little cloud, just beaming.

I am a long way from my home,
so far from the land of the free.
I do know how this little cloud feels,
a stranger amidst thousands of unfamiliar faces.

That little cloud is really alone,
as the stars light up the night,
the little cloud in it's own way
tries to blot out their light.

But try is all that it can do
and no more than that can anyone ask
as we face uneven odds
to complete our goals in this life.

That little cloud cannot hear or understand me,
but if it could I would say, "You are my friend,
you have given me respite
from all that awaits me come the morning."

Thanks ....

Simplicity

All of this seems so simple right now.
I fly there,
I get off of the plane and do my job.

I wonder, in the next few days,
if I will feel that smart
or feel that secure about who I am.

Oh I have seen people die,
but not killed or being killed.
I have never seen anyone tortured.

I have seen war movies,
but I have not been the target
for anyone wanting to shoot at me.

I have hiked for days before,
but not for the purpose
of destroying everyone and everything.

I have been trained to understand war,
but still I guess the understanding
comes from being there.

Here tonight on this trip to there,
life seems so simple,
I wonder when the time comes for me to go home

if I will have witnessed only simplicity.

Preparation For It

My mind seems to bounce from one thing to another,
as I try to understand
just what is out there waiting for me.

I have very little knowledge of war,
but then I am, in my heart,
not a warrior, but rather a healer.

There is nothing that I can do
to get ready for what lies ahead for me,
but new classes in life start tomorrow.

So healer start to heal yourself,
make sure your supplies are worthy
of the trip that lays ahead.

Acquire plenty of things to occupy your mind,
plenty of strength to allow you to keep up
and above all faith in abundance

that you will always do the Big Healer's will.

PART TWO
"IT"

"It"

When I thought about coming to this place,
I never really knew just what "It" would be like.
There is no way that any one person can understand
except that he or she be right here in these boots.

Oh I had read about this place and these times,
but I had never come face to face with someone
who would take my life and never ask why
and then see someone that I know do the same to them.

I have never seen death on this level before
with no one to ask why or how,
just death with no questions asked
and no excuses called for, or needed.

The walking all the time is not so bad,
the bugs and all of the dirty days and nights
can be dealt with, in most situations,
but the death and loneliness of being here is punishing.

This is a long way from the soft pillows on my bed,
this is a million miles from the food my mother cooks
 and a lifetime for many away,
from ever going back to all those things ever again.

I have cried a lot since I got here,
but those tears are different than the ones I remember
when I said goodbye to a loved one in sadness
or stood for hours at my father's grave side.

These tears here are for people I never knew
who just in the prime of their young lives,
and in the middle of God only knows where,
were stopped from pursuing their dreams.

I would have never believed that there would be a time
when all of this life and death battling
would mount such an offensive,
that even time would have to stop and take notice.

I could only have imagined what this would be like
and because I was lacking in knowledge,
I never even came close in supposing
how this time would be for everyone here.

I must continue on now for there are other things
to be aware of in this day and the days ahead.
One day I hope to look back on all of this
and remember just how small I feel, just now in the midst of "It."

The Captain's Hole

His face was covered with dirt and the dirt was cracking.
I noticed the bars on his lapel.
"Captain how are you doing,
where have you been?"

The tears started rolling down from his eyes
and as they did they tracked down his cheeks.
They made a path through the caked clay
that covered most of his face.

"I can't take it anymore, I have had it,
I want to go home and see my family.
I do not want to die here in this place,
full of bugs and snakes and the smell of death."

He was a deserter and was fed up with everything,
that has pained so many before and after him.
I put my arms around him and he continued to cry
and took my arm and pulled me with him toward the west.

We walked for at least ten minutes
and there at the end of the runway,
was a hole, with a few items of food in it.
"This is my home, you are welcome."

He had decided one month before, that at all cost
he would spend the rest of his time,
in that awful place in a hole in the ground,
instead of taking a chance on not living.

"Today," he said with a smile, "I am going home
and I don't care how I look or how I smell.
I am getting on that plane
and I am going home, away from this hell hole."

Later I watched him as he walked up the ramp
and into the plane that would take him
back to some kind of place away from here,
then and only then would he be at peace and clean.

As I walked away from that time I thought,
what a way to be introduced to this place
and what a way for me to hear about this war,
on my first day in this place called Vietnam.

Love and Hate

There is a great deal of difference
some people say between love and hate.
Here in this place there are both
and I have fathered them.

There is a desire to never hurt anyone again,
but there is also the desire to survive.
There is the desire to seek revenge
when we see a friend die.

Love and hate seem to run full bore here
in times that are different, like love and hate.
The reality of that is very painful for me,
for I have never really hated before.

In trying to understand the two feelings
I am able to better understand myself
and all of the things that seem to run wild
through my head and heart.

I do not want to hate and yet
that feeling keeps me aware that in so doing,
I might better be able to survive
this whole time in my life.

Looking into the face of a friend who has died
causes a great deal of anger to be born,
but a stark awakening to the fact
that he could be looking at me.

Life seems so filled with folly many times,
of course that was a great many yesterdays ago,
now it could not be more valuable,
realizing that it could end with one squeeze.

We here hate and we love.
We love those around us
and hate those who seem
to keep coming at us.

We know them not, the enemy,
but they represent something
that is negative to our survival
and life is more important than before.

There is not much difference to me
between love and hate,
just a minute or two
or whatever it takes to end this plateau.

We can hate someone one minute
and then look at them laying there,
with life no more in them
and we feel some love come and some hate leave.

Who Is Guilty?

I have no way of justifying this mess
that seems to take every waking moment from us
and even some of the time
when we are shut down for sleeping.

We were sent here to do a job
and back home there are those
who will forever hold us guilty
of making this war an endless horror.

When and if I get home from this place,
I will never be able to say that I agree
with this war and all its toll,
but I will be able to say that I was called and I went.

Some will say that I was not smart enough,
or that I should have gone away and hid
or I should have just said no,
when the country of my birth called on me.

It is so easy to ask questions
when you are involved in no way here
with this time in my life
and when you are not involved in this hole in history.

It is easy to tell others how they should feel
about something that can only be known
if indeed you have witnessed it
in your life and in your eyes and heart.

No I cannot justify this war,
I cannot say that these deaths of the enemy
are happening for a righteous cause,
when those who started this war are getting richer.

You who would call me a thousand names
have seen fit to keep us here
by casting your ballots for those who started this mess
and have kept it going with your support.

I often sit here thinking of those
who have spent their years to present
making sure that the world does not forget this mess
when there are millions here who will not forget.

I may be guilty because I came here
or they may be innocent because they stayed away
from this time that will change
millions of lives forever ....

Who needs to justify their existence?

Understand Me Now

Life is so easy when time is not short,
when all that matters is food and a place to sleep.
Those things still matter to me now,
but life is different than it was before.

For some life is no more, period;
for others it is filled with tears and anguish.
That is what war does to its children
and we here are the children of this war.

We are the ones whose lives will be changed,
maybe for the rest of our lives.
I will be changed because I have seen the faces
of so many who will never see another sunset.

Some people have a way of understanding all of this
and then there are others who care not to try.
Life is truly easy when all we have to do
is think about what to do tomorrow.

Here, there may not be a tomorrow for some,
maybe not even for me.
I remember some who have gone ahead
to prepare a place for others to follow.

All of this might sound a bit dark,
well this is a dark place and a dark situation
filled with dark temperament,
that will not change for a while.

I am glad, in a strange way that I am here
and I will be glad to go away from this place.
Life will mean more to me out there now
than it did before this place came into my life.

This time in my life has caused me
to reevaluate the concepts of life and death.
There is so much of it here
and we will have to live with it until we leave and longer.

Death means different things to different people,
just as life does,
but how we address those two levels, life and death,
determines how we will be when we are older and wiser.

IF WE GET TO BE EITHER ....

337 Days

This feeling is so different for me,
not like playing a football game
in front of a crowd of people,
but still I am nervous.

There is no way that one can prepare
for these feelings in my stomach.
Sometimes I think I am going to be sick,
other times I just want to run faster and faster.

I am so flooded with emotions
and I cannot understand all of them.
They run together and find a way
to cause me to feel so many things.

I don't know where to step or sit,
I am not sure which spot is safe.
I feel excitement and I feel frightened,
but no one can ever know the latter.

I saw my first dead body today.
People back home may not want to hear about it,
but that is how my day was,
how was yours?

Time seems to creep by so slowly in these days,
I must have been here for at least two months,
let me see I have written the days on my helmet,
wow 28 days is just short of two months.

I have been told that I will get used to this,
so far that has not happened,
but there are goals out there for me to shoot for.
There are only 337 days left to go ......

The Sins Of This Place

The sin of this place and this war
is not that we are here in this awful place,
but that someone decided for us
that we should be here and play at this deadly game.

There is no way that I can justify this war,
these lives that are snuffed out each day
and the destruction that occurs in families
throughout this part of the world.

So often I sit and wonder who will
be held accountable in the final analysis
for all of this that has happened,
inside and outside of my own being.

Someone will have to pay for what is happening here,
someone will have to be the one who says
that the fault of this war
is not with the young warriors, but with others somewhere.

The Bible says that the sins
of one generation will be visited on another
and that will happen one day
and the world will know that we are and are not guilty.

The greatest crisis that we will have to face,
as we remember those that died here,
is to recall all of the things
that we have done in this place.

It will not be those who struck this war
that will cause us to have sleepless nights,
but rather those to whom we brought this war
and those whose lives ended in the drama being played out.

The sins indeed, after thoughts out of control,
are that we are guilty of what we have done here
and the years ahead will cause a great deal of pain,
when we try to forget that we were here.

Someone should share this blame with me,
someone has to remember that they pushed the buttons,
someone there must know that they bought my ticket,
but most likely we will stand alone and history will forget.

Happiness

When I close my eyes, a smile comes to me
for I see her face looking back at me,
her eyes are flashing,
smiling back at me from the other side of my eyes.

I cannot remember when last I closed my eyes
and her face was not there looking at me.
It is like a torch that will never go out
as long as this place in my heart is full.

Walking through this jungle day after day,
the hot July sun feels like an oven,
yet with all of this around me that is negative,
inside of my mother's son, somewhere

there is happiness ......

Tomorrow

I feel as though in this time,
this life has very little meaning,
except that right now in this moment
there is peace.

I am happy that there is this time of peace
and as I wrestle with my feelings
about things like being here,
I do have dominion over my mind's direction.

What else is there? One could ask
of the people who sit and wait,
seeking only from the present
and not looking to that time waiting out there.

I do understand today for I am here,
I recall some of the yesterdays,
but they are all one by one moving away,
so all that awaits for me is tomorrow.

In it can be joy and hope
even though in this hour there is uncertainty.
All of this questioning causes me to wonder
if peace of mind, for some, will ever come.

Still I know that at least for now
I live in this place and time,
that can be good or bad,
but it is good to know that I <u>LIVE</u> in this time.

For many who are here, this is a strange time
because in the midst of war there is peace.
Still my mind is muddled trying to understand
that I have control over some things,

but not over TOMORROW ......

Lord Have I Cried

I wish I could have talked to you yesterday,
you knew it was my birthday,
but I know the tears in your voice
would have caused me a great deal of pain.

Here in this war, in this place
neither of which I understand,
I am facing a foe, I am told he is a foe,
who I will never know.

I can remember the touch of your hand,
I can feel you in my very soul.
It seems those things that make me feel warm
are a million miles away from here.

Times and smiles here make very little difference,
except to create a place to hide
all of the things I have seen,
which keep my mind busy.

Here it is not easy to show tears.
Though many cry inside their private worlds,
they would not understand my tears
and how I feel when I see all of this and think of you.

Each of us, in our own way,
has to cry the way that heals ourselves
and all of the mess that gathers inside of us
The Lord knows I have cried ......

A Lifetime Since Yesterday

Time may never find us again
as it has on this very day.
We are cold, wet and homesick
and we have no patience or time for either.

Still they creep inside of all of us
like the wind blowing through a broken window
and we are left with only each other
and a thousand faces and memories of yesterday.

Though we will recall their faces,
their names will likely fade away,
but the death and the anger
will find a place to stay.

In the years ahead the reality of birth
will never mean more than it does right now.
Time will never forget us
and here we age as if time was in full throttle.

We all chase dreams,
when we take the time to think
about all of the things happening
in this part of our world.

We must continue to chase them,
but we have to understand the real times
and in all of this mental waxing and waning,
realize that we have lived a lifetime since yesterday.

That has been a short time for many here ......

It Is Better To Care

When the time comes for me to finish
this chapter in the story of my life,
I will go without hesitation into that day
for my burdens have been lightened.

But right now I sit here recalling
all of the tears that I have cried
and even the few smiles which have been birthed
in this place so far away from my home.

I can see the faces of people who I have known,
some of them are still alive,
they are all part of me
in some strange participatory manner.

I remember the faces of little children,
some of them badly burned,
the hungry and the prosperous,
the sunrise and a million stars after the rain.

Truly I will recall most of these things
until the final chapter of my life has been written,
for they have helped me to realize
that it is better to care than not.

Mine

The clouds are moving around rapidly,
they have colors mixed all together,
as the wind tosses them here and there
the sun makes them look like pillows.

This day is nearly over,
the rains have come and gone,
I feel as if I can breathe again
and enjoy a night's rest.

This endless jungle here for a long time,
has been the home for trees and animals,
but that was before man decided
to change their fate.

As the clouds seem to splinter and depart
and the sun is heading for the other side of the world,
all of this will in a few hours
be only a memory.

Yet as all of this happens
the far away world will not be concerned,
except a few who remember I am here,
so I will call this time and place mine.

For Richard

As I look around in the silence of this time
I realize that this is a time for tears.
It is also a time to remember how good it is
to care about someone.
Right now death seems so final,
when the hour comes to say goodbye
to a friend that we only knew as Richard.

We do not need to say trite words
for they do not mean very much here.
We do not have to stumble over sentiment
when there is no history to talk about.

His face and the glow of that picture,
which has been captured in our minds,
will remind us for many years
of someone each of us in our own way loved.

The ray of light which surrounds his memory
is filled with the good things he shared with us.
I hope that even unto death
he knew that we loved him.

If he did then I can only pray
that the knowledge of that love
made his journey
into his new life an easier one.
We sit here gathered, wondering many things,
but I am aware of the reality of eternal life
and at this moment for Richard I am glad that is a reality.

Where Will It Stop?

I sat today on a mountain top seeing the world below on fire,
wondering when and where it will all stop,
this hate that seems to grow day after day.

I really believe that the mountains were made
for people to come to them and feel enriched,
so their joy might be uninterrupted.

I looked down on this sight and I knew
that God's children would quarrel again
and some would never see the rising of the new sun.

Here sometimes it seems so serene to these eyes of mine,
it seems so peaceful
and then the sounds of reality awaken me from my sleepless dream.

It is too bad that all of this beauty is wasted on man,
why that has happened is more than I can comprehend.
It seems some strict ban is needed to remember who is in charge.

Yes, I sat there on that peak watching the jungle below
wondering if man will ever create peace of mind
and avoid his fear of failing.

That peace can only come when people are felt to be kin,
when we seek to be family and not foe
and when we seek from the weak the same as we seek from the strong.

Beauty I would love to see, but below there is pain
and the tales that the miles sometimes hide
are a reality to me in this hour.

People who we do not know except that they be the enemy
can never come together with us in a common plea,
unless we stand side by side and listen to each other.

Then we can find a peace that is real
and the sounds of war will cease in this place
and banners of hope will ride in the wind.

Then and only then all of this might stop, ...

I Don't Know

Listening to this rain, I wonder if I will ever
get out from under this poncho.
Oh, yes, there are tears out here and fear,
also questions of necessary matter.
Men talking like they are strong and weak,
some minds are scrambled and some are clear.

We are having to let friends go,
day after day
and that alone takes it's toll.
While some seem to be able to forget,
others seem to always remember their faces
time and time again
and the tears come without advance notice.

The rain is still falling on me.
No one seems to know why we are here.
No one seems to know what is ahead, only what's behind.
I surely do not know why we are here
or what lies ahead for any of us in particular.

I just know that misery and sadness seem to take center stage
in my life right now.
This is not how I was when I came here.
When will I be able to laugh again from sheer joy?
I have no idea about all of that,
only all of this.

I know that out there,
in what some people here
call tomorrow, I will laugh again,
but it seems so far away from here.

So many have gone away and left us,
gone far away.
Will we remember them come that illusive tomorrow?
Some I am sure will forever
touch the pure fibers of my mind by memory
and others,
I don't know, I just don't know.

Somewhere In Southeast Asia

We gathered there today to remember,
yes, to remember those who gave all they could
for their nation ......
Many places around the world are in turmoil,
yet in this place today,
for this time there is peace ......
Peace is far deeper than nations shedding
their arms of death and destruction.
Peace is far more noble
than having all social strife eliminated.
Peace is much greater than familial harmony.
Peace can exist inside of each person
who understands the value of life.
We can have peace when we join hands and hearts
with people around the world.
It only takes one person talking to one more person
to start a trend for peace
or just someone talking to himself,
like I am doing right now,
remembering those that we came here to remember.
All they had to give was their life
and that they did.
Maybe someone back home will remember them.
I know that I will,
if not by name, by face and place ......

Memories

People come into my life
at a rate faster than hearts can allow
and most of them disappear
before I even know their names.

It is not hard to be a hero here,
there are many and there are few,
for they all think of others
and the feelings of being a hero are lost.

It is not hard to be a clown here
for that saves many a day from being lost,
when all that is seen
is the awful mess of death.

Being heroes and clowns
can drain the heart of emotion,
but that is an avenue of survival,
for being alone here can drag anyone down.

All of these remembrances
of nameless faces taken away
in the height of their short lives
causes a great deal of pain here and at home.

Slowly through all of this,
their expressions fade away,
as does the time that they were here,
but never does the memory of them abandon me.

Just Love Her More

This emptiness I feel just now inside of me
is only a reflection of all the emptiness and pain
I see and hear all around me.

Oh, yes, there is laughter here and there,
from the hearts who are young in hours spent here
and less than weary from these surroundings.

I yearn to once again walk in the ocean,
to see the waves curl and fall at my feet,
to wipe the spray out of my eyes, reddened by salt.

I cannot know in this place and time the joys of love,
for the one that I love is so far away from me,
sleeping just now and dreaming of many things.

I know that she stopped today and said a prayer,
to ask God to watch over me,
knowing that through the miles it was heard.

It has been an ageless concept, this timeless love,
how sweet it is when two people find a path together,
just now the sweetness seems to taste different somehow.

But I know that if I ever get out of this place
and come face to face with her again
I would not try to change her,

JUST LOVE HER MORE ......

Important

This is a strange place
and people seem to worry over weird things,
yet other elements seem to be
of more importance to me.

It is important what I feel inside of me,
as is the hatred I see in the eyes of young men.
The loneliness is important
and important too is the death of innocence.

It is not important how we got here,
it is not important who we hurt today
or what we did today, maybe one day they will be,
but what is important is the death of innocence.

So many here have no idea
what this day really meant to them.
They just think of the morning
and where they would like to be at its birth.

What is important is what a person really is.
We are here all together in this place
and God only knows how we got here and why.
What is important is that one day we will be elsewhere.

The years will come and I hope they will go,
yet the fragments of this time will burn
like a flame around a funeral pyre
and then the death of innocence will be observed.

Scales

As I watched from not so far away,
the sun was beating down on me
like a hot iron and I was wet, totally wet.

I knew why I was feeling that way
and as I watched I could feel my insides
turning faster than the speed of sound
until they just stopped and like me were all used up.

I walked over and helped lift the bags
and one after the other we placed them
in their own spot on the chopper,
ready for transportation to another stop.

One after the other, time and time again
we lifted the bags up
and I felt weaker with each one,
until the task was finished.

All I could think about that night,
as I laid there under the stars
and remembered what that day had been,
was I never knew how heavy dead bodies could be.

Time seems to drift by me now
and the memories of that day are out of focus,
except I seem to recall over and over again
the weight of the bodies as we lifted them up.

It is not strange to me
that I remember that time, but not where and when
all of that happened,
just the remembrance of the weight

and how that hour and the weight of the bodies
imposed on my soul
and of course my heart ...... vivid pictures.

A Mother's Tears

How many times has the thought echoed in my mind
about the tears and pain which must be shared
by so many mothers whose sons will never come home?

Each day brings new sights and therefore awakenings,
and they are followed by memories,
because each day the touch of death has been felt so closely.

I know that my mother would never stop grieving
if by some chance or strange bullet,
my life would come to an end here.

So many things are going to happen in so many places
when this day is over finally
and the news of another day's tolls reach their destinations.

I hope someone is there to hold those mothers,
as they remember the little boys
who laughed and played and grew up for this.

Oh, I guess I am a little bitter to know
that these young men might never sit by the river
and listen to the sounds of the rushing water at nightfall.

They will never walk with their lady love,
they will never just be at home
and be filled with all of the smells of that place.

So, as the tears fall from your cheeks, Dear Mothers,
I wish all of us here could get together and hold you tightly
and let you know that we too have lost your sons.

Our loss can never be as deep as yours is,
for you are a mother to someone who will never come home,
but remember that we too, have in our own way, lost your sons ......

Returning Is Good

In all parts of this little bit of the world,
war rages and turmoil persists.
All over this land people are firing up the horizons
and have given history credence.

Still in view of all of this,
people do not want to war against each other.
They want to put away bitterness and stress
and bring friendship and brotherhood out of the rain.

And at this time of the year when children
wait the coming of Christmas morning,
we have laid aside our weapons of war
and for this day there is peace.

Tonight the sound of "Silent Night" will ring out
and indeed it shall be that,
for even those who are here without God
are out there somewhere and there is quiet everywhere.

All of this hope abounds here because
many years ago a child was born
and with that birth came a message of hope and love
and now that message rings loudly in the silence of this peace.

So in our gathering together
we must give thanks that there is no death and war,
and in this quiet time,
we can remember things that will never be forgotten.

As we sit down together and recall other Christmas Days,
as we sing these wonderful Christmas Carols,
let us remember those not here and those

who are wounded,
who are sick,
who are afraid,
who are in pain,
who are alone,
who are in this with us,
and those who have died.

If we come to this time in our lives
and try to return this time to it's intended meaning,
then this day will be a true joyous Christmas
and the days ahead will be different for all of us

and of course for me.

Christmas ('68) A Time For Me To Remember

My mind is warmly tangled with memories
of years and yuletide seasons past,
of prayers for peace and a hope for that peace,
to be realized in my lifetime.

So another season of love rolls around
and once again we grip the reality
of cold nights and hard days of walking,
to make salvation on this plane possible.

But somehow the measure of all of this,
at least in my mind,
is seen in the ability to make it through these long days,
looking forward to a warming fire under my poncho out of the rain.

I hope this season will once again bring me to the brink
of truly understanding what Christmas is all about.
I hope we all here understand that though we be tired and dirty,
we are all loved and cared about.

Once this season's hope grasps me
I want to be able, in my own way,
to plunge headlong and heartfelt into all the emotion and joy
that was intended to be Christmas.

My prayers, as always, are for peace inside of me and out
and I pray that we here never lose
that feeling of hope in our hearts
for better times than these, close to the ones we love.

That in itself is the level of knowledge and security
that separates those of us who celebrate Christmas;
as the birth of love and mercy and therefore forgiveness,
from those who just celebrate the holiday.

This holiday, though it is a strange place to be, is special
for I have been thrown together with many new friends
and this is our first Christmas together
and I pray it will be our last together.

As we have gathered here today, the guns of war have been silenced
and this holy season has gripped some of God's people.
The recognition of the birth of the Christ Child
has been accomplished and truly in this hour there is peace.

As I observe people come and in their own way they worship,
I hope their families remember how much love means to them,
especially on this day,
when families are together at least for a time.

As we sit here away from the sounds of the war for a while,
we are emotionally safe in the memories of loved ones far away.
For the rest of my life, be that time short or long,
this Christmas will be for me a SPECIAL TIME TO REMEMBER.

New Year's Eve

Everyone is sitting around like every other night
and indeed here it is like every other night,
but it is New Year's Eve,
this year is rapidly coming to a close.

We are almost running out of 1968
and needing to ready ourselves for 1969.
I have to chuckle a bit,
for it sounds like a wine list of sorts.

The good thing about this year going away
is that we made it through it
and have the possibility
of fully facing another one ahead.

We have been lucky as this year rolls by
and of course all of that is relative
to what others have been through,
maybe that will continue to be our trek.

As this new year slips into it's own,
I cannot help but to whisper a prayer,
for so many who have been touched
by the pain of this place and this war.

Yet the new year will bring us closer
to going home and getting away
from this place, these people
and this war that has already claimed too many ......

Time Is Up

"Hey, I only have 135 days left and I am out of here.
The end to this part of my life is just around the corner.
I will be a free man once again,
watch out Motown cause here I come.

Oh, yes we mark time on the calenders at home
and on the desk where we work
and here on the helmets that we wear,
each and every day of our lives.

Thinking of going home from this place
can generate such a feeling of hope,
that it is hard to imagine,
unless someone has been here and seen all of this.

No more of this filth to fill my brain,
no more of this food to almost fill my belly,
no more of this cold, wet drama
to keep me awake every night.

I cannot change what is behind me,
I cannot change all of this that has changed me,
but I can change what is out there,
in that day when I walk away from this place.

I may have to be alone for a while,
when I get back to that world I left before
and that will be alright,
at least I hope that it will be alright.

When the time comes for my life to end,
I want to be somewhere far away from this place
and with someone who cares about how I breathe
those last valuable breaths."

That was two days ago now,
when I heard that young man speak those words.
I wonder where he is,
I hope he is alright and moving along with 133 days to go.

The Traitor

They talk about him everyday
and they know that he is a traitor
and yet each day he leads us out
into the bush and maybe into the hands of his friends.

I cannot understand all of this,
maybe they are smarter than we think,
the officers who make the decisions,
but I do not believe that is the case.

I have watched him for days
and each time he seems to be alright
and yet we continue to suspect him
of leading us into danger.

We lost someone yesterday
and that has a great many of us uneasy,
but that was then
and we have to be concerned about now.

Shots are being fired up there,
something is happening.
I wonder just what is going on,
we will find out soon enough.

Now the day is over
and the bad news came our way.
We lost another man today and what of this lesson,
that seems so hard for many to understand?

Must try to sleep,
for there is much to do come the morning
and when it comes issues to be settled,
about times and hours past and present.

There will be no more ambushes we have been told
and as this greeted me,
the early morning light
came crashing into my eyes.

Having this greet me
was a strange way to wake up
and yet making sense of it,
was all the more moving.

The whispers flew through the company
like the wild northwest wind
and they carried the message
that the traitor had died in his sleep.

No one said anything about it,
but we all knew
that his sleep had not killed him,
but his diligence to duty had ......

Sacred Trees Are Planted There

It seemed so quiet for a brief moment,
away from all of the sounds that war makes
and then as if the world had exploded again
an old man came running toward us.

His hands were waving back and forth
and his voice was loud and high pitched,
screaming in Vietnamese,
what seemed to be screams of horror.

Someone grabbed the old man,
searched him and tried to give him water to drink.
But he would have none of that
and continued to wave for us to leave.

No one could understand his dilemma
and so the verbal bout continued
for what seemed to be a long time,
then in desperation the little old man fell to the ground.

As he lay there on the ground still screaming
and the tears were rushing from his eyes,
he never moved from that spot
and then someone made sense of all of it.

We were sleeping in an area, reserved for many years
for burials of famous and respected holy men
whose honor and memories were kept alive by this place,
this little space of treed land.

Slowly we moved away from that spot
and slowly his tears passed
and he sat up in the middle of the garden,
as if to feel that the spirits were again resting.

There is something to be learned from this
I thought to myself as we walked away from that place.
The memories of those who we love and revere
are very special and nothing, not even war

SHOULD CAUSE THAT TO CHANGE ......

The Old Couple

The village was empty except for two old people.
As we walked through the burning little town
nothing that we did caused the two old people
to even move so much as a muscle.

They watched us as we moved very slowly
in and out of the burned out huts,
making sure that the old people
were indeed alone in that place.

They knew that they were going to die,
they just did not know when that would happen
and they did not know how it would happen
or which one of us would kill them.

There was no fear in their eyes.
There seemed to be nothing that would make them move
from their squatting position,
that was now very familiar to each of us.

I wondered what they were seeing as they watched
as these strangers came crashing into their lives,
not caring about them
and how they would be tomorrow.

"They could be V.C.," someone shouted.
"Maybe we should search them," still another said.
"Hell, let's kill them," screamed a third
who was caught up in the fire of war's emotion.

"They are alright, leave them alone."
Was the sound reason in that hour.
"They are just old people,
if you are lucky maybe you will be old one day."

As we made our way through the village,
on the way to that next place,
I turned and the old couple were still sitting there,
as if to say that they would die before they would move.

I probably will never forget them,
for I too would have rather died than given up,
everything that I had known for at least eighty years.
When that is gone there is only death ......

Waking Up

This is a rare world into which I awoke this morning.
It makes no difference here who we are,
what our names might be,
our color or our physical appearance.

There could come a time when a round
from a gun of someone who knows us not,
could take my life
or the life of that young man to my left.

Those bullets do not discriminate against anyone
and in these hours discrimination,
on that level is not only acceptable,
but in most cases preferred.

My job here is to bring about some sense of healing
and to this date
there seems to be a great deal of need
for my work to continue here.

In this place one wonders and dreams
about a great many things away from here,
but in the time I have for solitude,
I think of ways to make this place better.

I guess in a universal way
I worry about the families of the enemy,
knowing that they do not understand me or this war,
and I am not sure I understand either myself.

These men are so frightened and so alone
and yet they act as if nothing is wrong.
Then in a moment of humanity,
the walls come tumbling down.

They may never feel this vulnerable again,
because in that feeling there is danger
that they could get hurt,
even more than they have been by their losses here.

These boys will be men when they leave here,
they will have witnessed the end of life,
they will have witnessed the birth of hate
and they will have memories for a lifetime.

This is a rare world into which I awoke this morning.
It makes no difference who we are,
it only matters that we are here and alive,
for there are others from just last night,

who were not so lucky, their name was on the bullet ......

The Memorial Service

We gathered in that place, as many as a hundred or more,
to say good-by to three who left us the day before.

There were a lot of dirty faces
and most of them had tears in their eyes.

"We have come here to say goodbye to three comrades
who left this life serving their country."

All heads were bowed, not in prayer, for the most part,
but in pain and the emotional ache of not understanding.

My understanding is that war has given to me
a basic realization of the value of unity.

We have it here and we need it too,
for without it there is little chance of survival.

That day as we said our goodbyes to the three;
Dawson, Frankwitz and Ricardo, I was given new feelings.

They all came from different religious backgrounds
and yet we came together to say, "safe journey."

Our prayers are for them,
to one God, Who created us all.

He, Himself, must have times
when He also sheds a few tears of pain.

as He watches His children rolling around
in pain and abandonment.

I hope that their families knew that somewhere
in the middle of all of that hell

a group of ratty looking young men,
said farewell to their sons and were hurting too.

Young Men In War

They look so young, these young men at war.
Before the next sunrise any one of them
might not be able to express the way
he feels about this place and time in his life.
They come from everywhere
to this place,
to fight a war,
that no one really understands,
at least no one in this country.
Some of them laugh,
some of them cry,
but only in the quiet moments,
when their hearts cry out
for all those things
that were not very important,
when they were free and an everyday experience.
Times sure change,
as do the hearts and desires
of those people trapped
in a place without the creature pleasures,
of life and time.
The pain and the hunger
for better times,
can easily be seen
in a furrowed brow
and the heads hung low,
as if in prayer, but alas not so.
Prayer like crying is not the thing to do,
but one day in each life,
that will be accepted
by all of those here,
with no fear of ridicule
from peers,
who are all the same,
in more ways
than they can explain.

How Old Are You?

His hair was a red as the clay in north Georgia
and his freckles popped out like the new day.
It is too bad that he never got to see this new day
or to hear these words written about him.

He, like millions of others, was too young to be here
and too young to be caught up in something
that grown people decided was the thing to do,
in their time in history.

I wish I had known him a little better
and I could have found out about his life,
which seems to all who are standing here and watching,
to be over and done with, except in these few words.

I never knew how old he was and I never asked,
it seemed so insignificant at the time,
but so important to me right now,
he seems only a teenager.

Someone said that he looked like he was sleeping
and then they turned away from the reality,
that he was dead as dead could be,
never to smile again at family, friends or the boys.

So we write another letter to faceless people,
who will never remember the letter,
for it is only the final nail in the coffin of their son,
lost and gone forever, except in their memories.

It seems so useless, all of this dying ......

Be Real

How does it feel to hear someone say
how good you have done today
and all you feel is despair,
because the victory cup seems somewhat empty?

You were there when they needed you,
you reached out for them and you touched them,
you were an example of strength to them,
before they died.

When will we come face to face with the awesome facts,
that there is no room here on this earth
for anyone who cannot give a bit of themselves,
for the betterment of mankind?

Oh, yes, I have sat there and listened to them,
as they talked about their beliefs,
as they grappled for words to say,
about the ones they left behind.

I was there when letters came from home with pictures
of new babies and times around the Christmas tree.
I was there when those letters promoted tears
and I was there when the tears stopped.

I have been told how good it was that I was there,
when the stress of war became too great
and the mighty warriors felt their bellies hurt,
from the same fear that had gripped their fathers.

In being there I felt a bit small,
because the best is many times mixed with the worst.
I was also there with them when they breathed their last
and said a seemingly hollow prayer over them.

I will go on and do the best that I can,
knowing there will be times when that will suffice,
but there will also be times
when that falls far short of being enough.

It Is Only A Gook

The day seemed to be about the same as the others
and then it all changed, very quickly.
As I walked along there on the side of the road
was a dead person, dressed in black.

"It is only a gook," I heard someone say
and on we walked through the rain,
but all day I thought about the dead man
and how that moment might have changed my life.

I had seen dead people before,
I had watched people die even,
but probably not like that happened.
War is certainly different from all other places.

I have thought about that scene for a long time
and I realize that what I saw
was indeed what war is all about,
and what I saw was non living proof of war.

People come and they go,
but in this environment they go faster than sound
and that alone is hard to come to grips with,
because one day it might be someone that I know.

That would be no less painful for me
than for someone who had known
that little guy laying on the side of the road,
never to move, unless someone carries him away ......

Feed The Enemy

So many stories have been told of children
being abandoned in the very prime
of their young lives
and the person in my clothes understands that.

It is cold here only because the rain never seems to stop.
We have walked over half of this country
in search of what?
God only knows.

The people who sent us here have left us here
and the people back home think that we are evil for being here,
but the worst part of it all,
is the feeling that it will not change.

Today death touched us again
and the fighting continued off and on.
We followed the enemy to their camp
and we found where they had been eating.

That was not as important as what we found there.
The food that "Charlie" was eating,
the food that was nourishing the enemy, who could have killed me,
was sent to them from California.

It is bad enough to be here in this place,
without having to know that people,
who live in the country of my birth,
think so little of me that they would feed he who would kill me.

I have felt all kinds of new pain
since I stepped into this country.
I have seen death and I have been hungry
and I have been so cold in the heat of summer and it's rain.

I have been lonely for my family,
I have no idea just what lies around the bend
or what will come to me in the next new day.
All of these things pain me greatly.

Though they do cause me to sleep less,
they are not the bottom of the emotional barrel.
That position is reserved for the realization
that my people have decided to cast me out.

They have decided that I do not count,
so they have found a way to reach across the sea
and send supplies to those,
who in the wink of an eye, would take my life.

I am not sure if this pain will ever go away.
I am not sure if I can ever tell this story.
I am not sure anyone really cares about how I feel.
I do know that in my memory this event has found a burning home.

His Country

I would like to express my heart and mind,
yet in so doing I feel a bit of reluctance,
but the truth is all that I know is right here inside of me
and I do not want to hide that anymore.

But of course I will continue to do just that,
at least from many whom I meet.
The reality is that time will try to explain
this place and all that has happened here.

This all did happen and the future will be shaped because of it,
some may call this pleasure, but most think it is pain,
but I pray that before I die,
I will find some peace about this place.

I have walked a long way today,
I saw people die and others trying to survive,
but my heart may never feel more full than right now
in this quiet time of remembrance.

Oh, I guess it might be foolish to some,
for me to fret over the suffering
of some family here,
as they wade through the storm of their loss.

It is true that life with all of it's trails and tracks
has a great many more things to resolve,
but somehow in this moment of time
none are as painful as what is inside of my heart right now.

"All is fair in love and war," someone said
and though that is true they probably have not been here.
My mind still wonders about his family, wherever they are
and how they will be crushed by the knowledge of his death.

I would like to touch their hands,
wipe away their tears
and help them mourn the death of their father, husband and son,
who was only defending his country.

We here are lonely most of the time,
still there are times when that slips away
and we are graced by the sweet memory
of those back home who wait for us.

We leave somewhere different each day
and for the most part we choose not to remember times past.
It is like the first time we ever saw the moon full
and then forget that feeling once the moon has changed it's phase.

Stories will be told of these days and nights.
It is really hard to be away from home.
Yet, one of the hardest things for me to forget,
will be I am sure, that family, as I replay them, in loss.

It is not that I do not care about those around me
and the thousands of others seeking to end this madness,
but from this time forward wherever I go,
I will remember how I felt in this time of my life.

Love cannot last forever, so say the poets,
hate also will run it's time out
and just now watching this dead little man laying there,
I want to hold on to the love I feel inside of me.

I guess to some it might sound crazy,
but this war has brought me a certain peace.
I do not always understand all that happens to me,
but I do understand and realize what has happened to me here.

He lays there so still just now
and we will pass along and leave him, as we go our way.
His family will never know any of this
or that someone like me did shed a tear for their pain.

Their pain is no different from the pain in Iowa,
the tears they shed are no different from those cried in Vermont.
I feel so sad about this time,
when so many young men on both sides

have only today to live ......

Patriotism (over here)

Back home people are not talking about patriotism,
they used to talk about it a great deal,
but somehow with this war it has all changed;
too bad, for those feelings were good ones.

Children should grow up with feelings of pride
in their families and in their country.
They should understand the privilege
of being in a place where the people are revered.

For those of us here in this place,
being cast out and forgotten is a heavy load,
but one day, if we are fortunate,
we will return to that place called home.

Some of us will still be feeling
the need to salute the flag,
whenever it flies in front of us,
and a special pride swells our chest.

The strange part in that whole concept,
is that many of us over here feel that pride.
We are like family, many of us
and we are friends, a great many of us.

We have been brought together by this war,
we are thrown together by pain and despair,
but we are welded together, some of us,
by the fact that we are serving here for our country.

So when people down the road in years to come
talk about how it felt long ago to be patriotic,
I will have to smile,
because I will remember the way we are right now, some of us.

I guess tonight in parts of the good old U.S.A.
patriotism sleeps sound and hard,
but here there are many who will forever try
to keep that light burning as was the case ......

OVER TWO HUNDRED YEARS AGO ......

The Diary

Dear Diary, these are the quiet times,
when all of this seems to be tolerable,
in some weird manner or another.

Times when the firing has stopped
and with that halting in pain
has come a great deal of mind altering quiet.

When I take the time to think about things at home
and those people who love me,
it is the best part of each day.

Writing on your pages helps me
to understand how I feel about all of this,
that has filled and fractured my mind for months.

Thousands of visions run through the corners and cobwebs
of my mind in these times,
but feeling those rhythms is strangely comforting.

Some good things happened today,
the Lieutenant fell into the river
and we all had a good laugh at the little guy.

We make fun of him, but he is a good guy,
yet he will never hear that,
from any of us.

Well I had better close for now
and lay down here under these stars
and enjoy the peace and quiet.

Tomorrow is another day
and with it will come more news for you,
till then I am signing off.

May 1, 1969 ...... 233 days left ......

B.H.

The Diary (part two)

Dear Diary, This was another good day,
no one got killed or wounded
and Charlie was no where to be found.

The quiet seems strange two nights in a row,
but I will enjoy it,
for as long as I can get it.

No mail from home today,
but it will come tomorrow,
like always tomorrow is a great day.

In it there are dreams and fantasies,
there are times of release
and there is transportation out of this place.

The firing has started again,
I knew it was too good to be true.
Sooner or later it starts, this is war.

Well, I had better close for the rounds are getting closer
and I must take shelter
before ....

Deserted

It is hard for me not to be bitter,
about the way some people back home
have decided that they will deal
with these young men who were sent here,
to serve their nation,
because their nation called.

Oh, I get upset by people
who wave their banners
and scream about a war
that they only read about.
They only have one point of view
about this part of the world and my life.

But the thing that bothers me most,
are the people who watched as loved ones went to war
and after some time alone
they then decide to do something new
and in a letter addressed to "Dear John,"
the relationship ends.

Do not think for one minute
that these young men here are true blue,
for nearly all of them are the same,
promoting big business
and bringing into this world
thousands of babies to be fed.

The pain for me is very simple,
they are only being what they need to be
and so it would seem is the case
for those who saw them off to this war,
but why tell them this now,
why let them think about coming home to nothing?

It is all in some kind of mirror,
for we are all a bit guilty,
of shoving and pushing our feelings
on to others at our point of need.
It just seems hard to go on
or to think about loving someone new,

after being deserted and hurt ......

The Hospital

The rows seem to go on forever in that room
and I wondered how it would feel to be there,
sleeping on those soft white sheets.

Soon those thoughts were chased away from me
by the sights that my eyes fell upon,
of so many people laying in all those beds.

All of those young men were going home
and yet they were going to be different
for the rest of their lives because of the war.

Oh, it is indeed true that some will consider this place,
to be a safe haven from the steel of war,
but others will have their lives altered forever.

Some may not make it out of here alive,
indeed as I watch I am aware that at least one,
will not survive this place and time.

The sheet is placed over his face
and they are moving him from bed to gurney,
making room for someone new to take his place.

There are very few smiles
as they roll the gurney down the hallway
and most of the survivors just turn away.

Those who turned away, their expressions never changed,
but the faces of those who watched the gurney,
showed the strain of the hour.

My own insides were in turmoil
and I was touched by that time and place,
when first I visited the hospital.

Little did I know that within two months,
it would be my turn
and I would occupy a bed in that same room.

This Birthday

Today is my birthday, May 16, 1969.
There will be no party here today in this place.
This birthday will be different than all of the others.
I am away from all of those who know the date of my birth
and away from any who might care that today is my birthday.

It is not that they do not care here,
but other things take a bit of a priority
when it comes to what we or they have to do today.
Let me see, we have to survive
and each one of us has to try to live to that next birthday.

When I get home I will be one year older in time
and a hundred years older in experience.
I will have seen so many sights that never need to be reseen,
I have felt pain that I never want to feel again
and I have watched humanity
throw emotional stones at humanity and I have cried.

So as I softly sing happy birthday to myself
I will have to hold off on the happiness
until the clock of life ticks up May 16, 1970.
Then maybe I will be somewhere more comfortable
and in the presence of people who know
that today is my birthday.

This birthday will not be forgotten
for there are things here that are different
from the other birthdays before
and I pray from the ones that lay ahead for me.
I am alone, without a cake and loving family around me
and I am aging too fast for one year's birthday.

Highs And Lows

There are so many ways to see this place,
so many times to laugh and cry about.
It all comes and goes like a time machine
and we are never sure which side will shine.

Someone might fall into the river in the morning
and everyone will laugh
and then in the evening toward dark,
he might be dead and we will all feel like crying.

This place causes sleepless nights
and the need to catch up in the light hours.
There are times when we are sitting together
and times when we need to be alone.

These times will be remembered,
for we laughed and felt the need to cry,
one we did together and the other alone
and too many of us grew up too fast.

The stupidity of some officers,
who had only been soldiers for weeks
and how they wanted to fit in
and had no idea how to make that work.

I guess all of our lives are a bit like that,
one day we are happy,
the next we are engulfed in sadness,
because we are human

and filled with many reasons for ups and downs.

The Old Guy

They kept talking about the old guy,
as if the man was at least 60.
Then he walked into the bunker
and the old guy was pushing 30.

To them he was an old guy
and that made me feel like a fossil,
for he and I were both the same,
we were pushing 30.

There was something about this old guy,
that was different from most of the men
that I had seen in my short time
in that part of Southeast Asia.

It could have been the cracks in his face,
it could have been the look in his eyes,
it could have been the way that he moved,
but there was something definitely different.

Watching him move and never look up,
as if he was on some strange, secret caper,
it was eery to me,
that he never seemed to smile.

It only took a short time in that place
for me to realize
that the reason he seemed different,
was because he was different.

By the time I became aware of the reasons
that he was different,
I discovered another startling fact,
I too was a bit different than before.

He was different because he was wiser,
not necessarily was that wisdom for the better,
but he was wiser and his world
had convinced him that was how he would survive.

The old guy had gotten a lot older,
in the few months that he had been there,
for taking lives and beating off death
will make us old beyond our history.

A LOT OF OLD GUYS CAME HOME ......

The Children

The red sky and the blue sky
seem to come together at the end of this day.

The children, somewhere close to here,
must have their heads bowed and tears falling.

For some near and far this will be a time
when daddies might not come home to them.

The stars will soon appear
and the moon in it's chosen quarter.

They will greet another like me,
who will also remember times before the war.

A country at war is no place for children
and yet those who war have other plans.

These children bear the scars of this time,
a time when adults altered their lives.

In a few hours the sun will come again
and once again there will be war.

What do these children here in this country
or others in the wars before, know about war?

They only know that because of their days of war,
they are hurt inside and out for the rest of their lives.

They are caught, the children are ......

The Children's Eyes

"A thing of beauty," someone said as they pointed to the mountain.
"Yes," was the reply, "but there is more here than meets the eye."

There are beautiful things in this part of the world crushed by pain.
I know the latter is true for I see it in the children's eyes.

To climb a mountain, green to the sky and see waterfalls below,
yes, there is beauty here, but it is hard to see beyond the memories.

Beauty yes, but hard to see unless one clears his mind,
of all the things placed there by the sight and sounds of war.

Beauty is only skin deep, far beyond the green canopy,
beyond the sunset into night, behind the children's eyes.

Many have seen beauty here, as deep and dark as it might be,
but for most the beauty is that one day they will be gone.

To not have to climb these mountains or steal around in the night,
with no fear for life, only to love where you are.

The mountains are green with mystery and beauty, there is no doubt,
the sun rises and sets and some do not even care.

This place has become a prison of dreams and hopes,
some hold a desire to kill and some fear retaliation for deeds done.

The passage should be straight away from this place,
changes will come here, but not in some lifetimes.

A thing of beauty this nation under war, maybe to some,
but not in the eyes of the children.

Please Remember Me

It was a rainy muggy day when he said, "remember me."
I cannot believe that in this lifetime,
I will ever be able to forget that place and his face.

Oh, I will be able to forget the rains that fell that day,
but I will never be able to forget him laying there dying
and the way that I felt when life for him was no more.

These are strange times here now,
good things and bad things happening each and everyday,
but right now the bad things ring loudest in my head.

My mind will never forget that special day,
that time when I was to share a final moment
with someone I felt I had known forever, yet not so.

I reserve a special place inside of me,
for that time and those feelings and his face.
I think it is right that time will not allow me to forget.

"Remember me," he said to me
and I know that he never realized
that neither distance, time or people

would or could cause me to forget that place and time and his face.

I Knew You Would Be Here

The day was aglow with the new sunlight,
but the air was filled with the sounds
of gunfire and human expressions of pain and fear.

From place to place I ran,
with more than I could understand to do
and there all about me was the reality of this war.

"Over here," some cried out
and there in the midst of his day of dying,
was still another young face.

Someone who would never see his Mother again,
he would never again fish with his Dad
and never walk down the lane with Mary or Sue.

I reached down to his lifeless body
and under his head I placed my hand.
I could feel the warmth of his blood between my fingers.

As I prayed in that moment for God to intervene,
my prayer was interrupted by a voice
for his limp and lifeless body.

I looked at his face and there was a slight smile,
"I knew you would be here," he said,
"Thanks," and once again and for the last time he lay limp.

My eyes filled with tears then and now,
to think that I was placed in such a sacred place
to be with Richard when last he breathed.

In a place so far away from everything that he loved,
there he died away from everyone,
except a friend who he trusted to come to him.

"I knew you would be here,"
the words ring over and over in my mind,
when I think these weeks later that about that time,
 I realize I was given a perfect gift.

Growth Or Change?

These men are not killers,
they seem to be like little boys,
who have been told
that they can play with guns.

The sad part in all of this,
is that they will soon grow up
and with growth will come
the understanding of the end of life.

It might be their life,
that will rapidly come to an end
or it might be someone
who feels the fiery dart from their bow.

No one came here knowing,
just how it feels to kill someone
and yet they will soon find out
that life can vanish in the wink of an eye.

These little boys will leave here,
some in boxes,
some in groups
and some will leave alone and be happy there.
Before they were not killers
but for this time in their lives
they have had the opportunity to be so,
but when they leave, death is supposed to stay.

They came here, many untouched
by that part of the world that deals in death
and how that is dispensed,
they leave here smarter and hurting from their education.

These little boys with guns
will go home men from under fire.
That will have changed their lives forever
and they will never be able to retrieve their innocence.

Their innocence and their virginity
have both passed away in these hours
and in the passing there has been growth,
yes, in the midst of death some growth occurs

or was that just change ......

Survival

When we get home they will say we are insane
and they may be right,
for being here in the midst of this thing
is indeed an insane gesture of life.

I was not born to this heritage,
to listen each and every day
for the bullet that might kill,
the person to my right or left
or alas the person between the two of them.

Man was not created to witness such as this,
death, burned body parts,
confusion as to who we should fight
and if we are supposed to kill at all.

Another of the thousand questions,
which ring through my mind
at the speed of thought and faster.

Confusion over how proud
one feels to be a part of something,
that fills each person,
with the desire to climb a mountain
and then in the midst of all of that,
to feel an aching in the pit of your belly
because the life of the enemy
has to be taken away,
in order for us to survive.

Life and death seem to me
to be joined together
in a different bond than before.
Before, of course, was when death
was a stranger and out there somewhere.

Yet, today that dark cloud of out-thereness
is knocking constantly on our doors.

We may be insane
and for this time in our lives
that might be the key for
SURVIVAL ......

Today And Tomorrow

I talked to myself today
and as I did the rains continued to fall.
The drops ran down my face
and a life that once knew so much joy now knows sorrow.

As I rested here today,
noises came into my ears,
loud sounds of thunder and lightening,
making that time uneasy, for the rain had stopped.

I listened today
and as I did I heard unhappy sounds,
sounds of a world seemingly loud and angry,
breaking up my time of peace and silence.

Today was quite a day,
tomorrow I will rise to face another day
and yet when and if I do that
I will be little older, not in years

but because of TODAY.

The Chaplain

The day was dreary and overcast as I stepped off of the chopper
and it is hard to totally recall what greeted me.
There in front of me was a soldier with his head bowed
and to his right lay twenty bodies bagged.

His dirty face was streaked with tears.
The day was early, his time seemed to be at least
one hundred years and his dirty face
showed the strain of the lives that no longer lived in those bodies.

He needed someone to put their arms around him,
someone who could cry with him,
someone who could understand that he
had reached the end of his rope.

The man was a chaplain, a man of faith,
but this for him was the last straw
and at least for this time,
had broken the back of his faithfulness.

Then the questions came from the chaplain,
as from many before,
"Why does God let this happen, where is He?"
The same questions that had been asked a thousand times before.

We sat there together with dirty faces and heavy hearts,
remembering in silence all of our own pain
and how that pain has brought us to this point,
where we never think much about tomorrow.

Slowly the bodies were taken away
and with each went a prayer of delivery,
to whatever is out there for them.
It is too bad those prayers came a little late.

The rains kept falling and so did the tears
and as the day and pain slipped slowly away,
to a level where no more tears could escape,
then time just moved on for the chaplain and me.

Today is another day and the rains have stopped,
but those feeling that presented themselves
at the sight of bodies stacked high,
will never totally depart from me.

Those memories allow me a time in my day,
to remember how badly we treat each other
and what a waste it is to take the life of someone
and then try and understand the feelings of his family.

Today is another day and the rains have stopped,
but those feelings that presented themselves
at the sight of bodies stacked high,
will never totally depart from me ......

Where Is God?

Where is God? I have often been asked
and I do not always have the right answers.
The answers that might cure the anguish
which rides hard in the soul
of someone thrown into this mess,
without a faith to understand
that even in all of this somewhere,
God will find a way to make His presence known.

Those stories that I heard when I was a child
will not stand the test of this time,
when in the time it takes to change one's mind
life is no more
and death will claim that life is now gone.
Still the child inside of me wants to visualize
times that are better and more equal to caring.

I watched yesterday as the faces of young men
turned colors relative to their place of heart,
when the names of friends were read,
who no longer breathed this air.
Where is God in all of that?
The question has to come
and it never seems to fail to arrive.

Then later that night
when I hear the murmuring
of a lonely soul lost and afraid,
then at that moment I know
just where God is in all of this mess.
He is there visiting at that very moment
and as He registers His presence with that young man,
He also passes very graciously through my heart and mind.

I could tell you that God is in the trees,
that He is in the sunrises and sets,
that He is in all of the times
when we are filled with joy.
I could tell you that He is in the memories of loved ones,
that might give us enough order to survive this place.

God for me is right here inside of me.
Yes, it would be nice if God would not let all of this
darkness find a way through to fruition,
but that is not the way it is
for we have been given a choice,
to believe or not to believe,
according to our own relationship with him.
That relationship and its depth
is what will carry us through this time and place.

I have no real answers as to the whereabouts of God,
except that He is inside those of us,
who feel the delight in believing that He is there.
As I close my eyes just now
I see a young soldier, tired and dirty standing there.
I recall how he looked around
and how he took to his knees.

"Oh God, in this night if you will be with my family
as they lay down to sleep
that they may know through these miles
how much I love them and think about them.
Be with those who are family for my enemy,
that they too might understand love.
Oh God, I pray just now for peace.

There are those who walk mile after mile
to voice their opinions about this war,
help them to understand the truth,
that most of us have no love for it either
and no reasons for being here except that we were sent here
and we are doing our job
and that is our only excuse for being here.

And now God as I try to sleep,
allow me to be the very best that I can be
and come tomorrow allow me to be used
in places and times which reflect my belief in you.
No matter what happens tonight,
let your will be done
and give me the strength to accept that.
I pray that my faith will last ...... Amen."

I saw a tear rolling down his cheek as he looked around
and I knew just where God was.
He is right there in that young soldier's heart
filling him with all the hope possible,
for better times and safe journeys.
I guess I found an answer to that question after all,
time and time again,
when I watched from a distance and close and heard prayers,
mine and someone else's.

God is beauty and God is love,
those phrases from my childhood search for God ring loudly still.
Yet the answers then I never found until
I stopped and asked my dad.
"Yes, God is love." he said to me.
"The love I have for you and a million times more powerful than that."
Then it all seemed so simple to me,
just as it is right now, here in the presence of God.

My Faith Is Not Gone

These young men, one after the other have come to me
and each in his own way has asked the same question;
"Where is God in all of this mess?"
and I have stumble for the right answers, finding very few.

It is not like I have lost my faith,
it is not like I believe less than when I came here,
it is not that time has eroded my hopes built on my faith,
it is just that I would like to have the right answers for them and me.

Right answers mean a great deal to people like me,
for that allows me to be able to say without reservation,
that my God has found a place here
and therein He resides and He wants me to come to Him.

Yet with all of this death around me
and promises of more of that laying out there ahead,
one has to be human to the point of wanting and needing to know,
just where all of this leaves the faithful.

Back home we are a so called Christian nation
and in that concept we should love those around us
and yet our nation has sent it's young men here,
to kill or be killed and me to watch over it all happening.

I guess I will never have all of the answers for all of these queries
and I will never understand all of this,
by the time rest catches up with me tonight,
but still the questions come and I just need to know.

So God if you are listening to me,
I need your help in all of this mess
and I want to not be able to just keep the faith,
but I want to spread it around.

I am sure that like many other times in my life,
you will help me make some sense
out of all of this that is happening here,
and in so doing redig my faith channels about you.

I know that you are here because I can feel you each and every day,
I know you are here because these young men talk about you,
I know that you are here because you would not have gotten me to this place
and then left me alone to the wilds of this war.

I am glad you are here in whatever form you take,
because it gives me the chance to express to someone,
just how I feel about this place and these questions,
for which I seek answers time and time again.

The questions, like my faith, will go on through this lifetime ......

Day Dreams

As one goes into tomorrow,
he needs to think about yesterday.
Some of those memories can help keep him
from being totally alone.

Life's highway has been good,
this part of the journey is less than perfect
and when I close my eyes tonight
a hundred faces will cross over my fence.

Thoughts of home, mom,
the things my dad would have said to me,
all of those things are so far away,
still closing my eyes brings them closer.

Sitting here by this river,
my mind is certainly busy,
on voyages and travels,
any one of which can take me away from here.

When all of this is over
and circumstances allow changes,
I want to do things differently
or at least appreciate that I can.

I sit here thinking about yesterday
and that will never stop,
even when this day is yesterday,
I will recall this place and this time.

The Night

I wish someone could explain to me
the meaning of darkness and what I see.
For when I look into the darkness of the night
I am greeted by shroud of comfort, power and might.

You walk in your mind both near and far,
you watch the tail of a shooting star.
The night can become as bright as the noon,
when one beholds the circular moon.

I watch the stars so placid and fixed
and every so often a planet mixed,
wondering what adventure one can discern
about the night if he wants to learn.

It might sound a bit strange or maybe not,
but I sit and contemplate at night a lot.
I try to think what I would do or say
if I could walk on the milky way.

This night holds such an awesome peace,
while most life here seems given by lease.
I am not at all in that frame of mind
for from the darkness peace I find.

I remember as a very small lad,
I would sit and watch the sky with my dad.
I guess because of the way he cared for me,
the joy in the night was not hard for me to see.

All of those years pass so quickly by,
I feel a small tear born in my eye,
that was ago many years and a day
and in this night I am so far away.

People move around and fret in the dark,
they feel fear and dread so often stark.
All of this is so strange to me,
for like always tonight I feel somewhat free.

The warmth of this night is all around
and so often mine is the only sound.
I wish the others here would seek to find,
the night I know to be so kind.

I love the sun and the light of day
for many things to me they say,
but I truly love the stillness of the night,
because the world herein seems to loose its fight.

It is calm and so very still,
as if with love it just may find fill,
with all of this filling me and all around
the night comes just now with only my internal sound.

Be as it may to you or me,
I know the night has the key.
The key to a clear and happy mind,
if you seek peace in the night that you'll find.

The guns have ceased to fire and sound,
so has all of my mental rambling around.
I hear only now whispers in the night,
we are all glad for the absence of the light.

Tomorrow it starts all anew,
so many things and miles to do.
But that is still a good sleep away.
I pray this peaceful night brings a peaceful day.

Despair

My mind mounts to a peak sometimes
and it is there tonight
and I feel a desire to explode
into total despair.

This night has already claimed too many lives,
these eyes have witnessed too much pain
for one person to see in a lifetime,
let alone a single night's darkness.

This day as it began was greeted
with uncertainty and thoughts of a prayerful nature.
The sun came and went
and we felt the impact of the night.

With but one single sound
the night began to explode
and with the passing hours,
faces were dissolved into only memories.

I do not know why they are dead,
I surely do not know why they were chosen,
I only know that now they sleep forever
and it is time for me to think of deeds not yet done.

Sitting here tonight,
this is a lonesome place,
my feelings are flying around
and it started with that single sound.

I can only think of the families,
there and here,
who will have to go through the motions
of missing and grieving over children lost.

Therein is the quandary that clutters my mind
in the midst of this week old night causing it
to explode into a many colored array
of feelings of need and despair.

A Word Of Thanks

In the midst of all of this turmoil and fear,
a message has been given to me.
Everyone around has had their say.
They only talk about things of this place and time.

I live my life with each new breath,
swear to myself to go from day to day
with a feeling that tomorrow will really come
and in this hour I have been rewarded.

I know the truth about this life,
I have felt my share of its loneliness.
My world is in great turmoil,
for we are at war with someone.

Yet, in the midst of all of this emotional trash,
in a time when everyone seems so fearful,
something new has come into my mental space,
a thought about the freedoms that I have.

They will all come to me in time,
when I will no longer be afraid.
Afraid to face the doubts of place and self
and I will be able to understand what I am all about.

I want to understand and be unconfused
about what really makes life good.
I know that I will one day be at peace,
for I have been on this journey.

Thanks for being a friend to me in this hour of my life
and saying that "nothing is more important than this time with you."
Friends come to us in the right time in our lives for healing
and I will always be thankful, you came to me in this time of my life.

I Am Glad

As I sit here I am glad for many things,
so glad my heart feels free to sing.
It gets me past all of this death,
to a place where I can emotionally survive.

I am glad right now that my ears can hear,
when the pain starts up again that may not be true.
I am glad that my eyes can see,
that may not be true when my heart is full.

So many things that I am glad about
and being here so far from home,
none is more important
than sharing this time with friends.

So many times and things which speak of good fortune,
until I came to this place and yet maybe here too,
I have had my share
and it has always made me feel special. (To someone)

I do not know what courage I might have,
I may have the desire to be brave or the need to run,
all of this I have to trust to a power greater than myself
and to my mind which unlike the sun never seems to set.

I am glad that I am not part of history yet,
with so little known of me to these people here and to myself.
I would not like to have someone read empty words from cold pages over me
and not know just how I feel tonight.

I am glad I am not like those birds there,
too many hawks to elude.
When I was a child I so wanted to soar like a bird on high,
but now just to walk and talk seems enough for me.

I once thought that this life was so easy,
from beginning to the end, only a game.
Now I am older and as they say a bit wiser
and I realize that the rules have changed.

I am glad, in all of this, that I am not alone
and like some, who have no one to share their feelings.
I am glad that I have someone, who may one day forget my name,
but for this time will listen to my dreams for tomorrow.

There are many things I've wanted to be
and many places I needed to go
and I guess as time passes by
that will change a thousand times.

It feels good to be a man of pain and tears,
for one day they say that will help me understand
all of those around me and their pain.
I am glad that my day of pain has come already.

Joy sometimes eludes me here,
when I see all that is happening around me.
I am glad that I can be touched in my time of need
and in return I can reach out and touch another who cries.

I am glad for touching ......

Those At Home

Sitting here I am remembering those back home,
those who I have never seen with my eyes.
Those who think that I have no feelings
or that I might be some kind of monster.

I am glad they are not here in this place,
they should be home with their families
and I deserve to be there too,
if the times and circumstances were different.

The only thoughts that run around in my head
are the realizations that they do not know me
and yet they can without thinking,
suggest to all that I am without feelings.

I am the one who walks around in this crap,
day after day and night after night.
I sleep wherever I can find a place
and I never know if my prayer at night will be my last.

Someday they may understand that I am the one
who went to school with them,
who played football and baseball with them
and who might have been a good friend, if times were different.

They probably will never read these words,
for they feel any kind of relationship,
with any one of us might cause their lives
to be transformed from one level to another.

If I could see some of them now back there,
I would tell them how they have misjudged
many of these men, some already dead,
they will never know how this all ends.

Some of us are not the tops of our classes
and we have doubts about being here too,
and then we hear of the parades back home,
but can only remember someone spitting on us.

Someday I hope all of these men who have grown up here
will get a chance to go home, that is not likely,
but they want to return to the land of the free and the brave
and to the land of those who cast us adrift.

Believe, if you can, that these are not words of anger
as much as they are words of pain,
for we have been sent here to this place
and everyone, save a few, consider us to be dead.

The sad part of that is, truth will abide,
for there are those here who will be heading home come the morning
and they will never know
who was friend and who was foe.

So, please understand that we do not want you here
and we do not want to be here,
but you are not here and we are
till death or time do us part ......

Not Understandable

Man does not know, nor is he able to understand,
why things happen when and how they do.
To see a sunset against a sparsely clouded sky
is not something that lends itself to understanding.

Standing here on the edge of this glistening jungle,
at the beginning of a new day and never knowing
just what the next step might bring
or if that step will be good or bad.

That is like watching the end of life happening
or remembering someone saying, "I love you."
The answers to why all of these things come our way,
man is not able to find, no matter how hard he tries.

To feel a desire to be somewhere other than here,
to watch all of these things happening, save the dying,
and to not deal with all that happens,
causes a great deal of non-understanding.

We came here and we do not understand
all of this that is happening in our lives.
Someone has to know that these feelings are overwhelming,
someone has to know, maybe each other is all that we have.

We can be imprisoned here and blame other people
or we can try to escape and survive all of this.
We cannot beat nature, no matter how we fight,
but we can beat human nature.

I do not understand how all of this works
or how I will be when the dust of this place
finds room to settle or time to change me.
I only know that like right now, most likely

I will not understand at least for a while ......

Those Boxes

Watching her there I lost contact for a moment,
forgetting what this place is all about,
but in the middle of that daydream
I found myself truly in the middle of this time and place
and the reality of both was an eye opener to say the least.

The hospital was full
of so many young men,
all of them going home.
Some had very simple wounds,
while others would bear theirs forever.

She asked the young sailor
standing there,
to not place the ammo boxes
so close to the hospital,
for that could be a dangerous thing to do.

He kept trying to explain
his situation to the woman,
but she would have nothing to do with it
and continued to ask him to remove the boxes
and then a tear slowly crossed his cheek.

"These are not ammo boxes," he said to her
"they came from in there,"
and as the tears fell
he slowly turned and pointed
toward the hospital.

It was then and there
that she realized in great pain,
that the boxes contained
the remains of those young men,
who never left the hospital alive.

I would imagine that at that point,
with tears too falling across her cheeks,
she like me and the other younger man,
had lost her place in the world
and reality was forcing her into emotional disarray.

That is what this war has done here,
it causes the growth of suffering
and for many who never feel the cold steel of a trigger,
they do see and feel,
the end result of someone who has ......

The Building

The building was a large structure;
with doors on both ends and a few people
wandering around inside of it.

When I first saw that place
and then walked inside of the tin walls,
it will be impossible to explain how I felt.

I had seen other buildings before,
which were used for unbelievable tasks,
but this was to be a memory for a lifetime.

The bodies were stretched out forever,
none, if any, had clothing on their cold bodies
and the air just reeked of death.

All of these young soldiers,
going home after all of these months,
in this place and for what?

Some of them died in battle,
some of them died on the table
and others just died.

The people back home will not want to read this,
because it will remind them of their losses,
but their losses have been implanted in my soul.

I stood there for a moment,
trying to decide whether to leave or stay
and then I remembered those who fell around me.

The morgue is an awful place
to greet the morning,
but better for me than for those that I saw.

There they lay all lined up
as if they are practicing for their visit
to the final resting place ...

I hope it is a place of peace finally ......

The Journey Of Darkness

These hours are so confusing, first there is hope of peace,
then there is the reality of war raging right in front of me.
These journeys from light into darkness,
from tranquility to turmoil are mentally painful.

This time in my life is a time of darkness with no light
to lead me through whatever is out there.
This is indeed a journey of darkness
and the only way that I can work through it, is to survive it.

The journey is dark because therein are elements
which are totally foreign to me.
There are so many sides to this day, moving toward night,
grief, death, stress, fear and always there is rage.

These feelings and reactions are all things of the soul,
but they come from the dark side of the soul.
Whatever happened to the sunshine that came into my heart,
so many mornings before I stepped onto this planet's spot.

I want this journey to be over and this time to be gone,
from this place I want to flee as fast as I can
and rediscover that old, seldom seen spirit of hope,
which filled my life for so many years.

I am angry because I am here in this place,
but so many others here are far worse off than I am.
I am angry because this place and time in my history
has robbed me of so much that was me.

I want out of this valley of thunder and darkness
and I want to see the sunrise once again in the calm
of another place and time when I am surrounded
by elements of peace and hope that will touch me ever so softly.

These hours are confusing because they are new to me,
but they are becoming very old very fast, for they try very hard
to take away from me the things that I wish to keep
and once I rise out of this valley, I know they will be present once more.

There are things out there in the day that will be of darkness,
there are times when I might hide my eyes
and there are people who will try to take away from me
the sunshine that came before and after this journey.

So this journey of darkness must have an end,
there must be a time of sunshine out there somewhere.
Just now the thunder inside of me is quiet.
I only pray that it will last until spring ......

Gains And Losses

When and if I get to look back on this time in my life,
I will need to ask myself about the gains and losses.
The losses are easy and hard to remember, as are their faces,
and the times when I remember becoming something different.

The something that I became was not always good,
but maybe one day that might be over
and some of my past might fade away,
like a lot of other bad dreams.

I have gained a great deal from being here,
I have learned to live with people of all faiths
and even those who say they have no faith,
even though it has been said that foxholes have no faithless.

I have learned about survival,
I have learned how to live with hunger and loneliness,
I have learned to understand life
and the reality of death.

My gains have been important for me,
though when I am gone from this place,
the losses will most likely stick to my heart
like soft butter to warm toast.

I can hope that somewhere out there,
when everything about this place seems to settle
and I have the time to reflect on this hour,
I can remember this little time of self examination.

I will, without a doubt, never forget the losses
which I have suffered through in this time and their faces,
I hope my heart never hardens to the point
where I forget their supreme sacrifice.

But if I can live in the positives I will be able to survive
and maybe understand and make sense out of all of this
which at this point seems to be so senseless.
I guess in understanding my gains, I can understand the

worth of life ......

Death In Life

Sitting here this seems to be like death,
for this loneliness seems to kill,
maybe not my physical being,
but rather the emotions that create happiness.
Accused and realizing my crime,
I pay not in years
but rather in labored breaths,
for each one is done in pain.
Pain is seeing life destroyed,
of realizing that tomorrow
will be the same
and without chance of change
all will be as it is right now,
only a day later.
How long can this go on?
How long can one's mind
go swirling through days and nights
never knowing its destination?
Alone here, I think not,
others and God surround me.
He has chosen to make me free
and thus to think
and understand right and wrong.
So here we are,
all of us, so far from home
and suffering from this place.
My thoughts are everywhere.
Everywhere, even here,
within this flimsy existence.
In reality I will awaken
and find myself unennobly entombed.
This death will one day stop,
my loneliness may or may not continue,
for when I leave this place
I go to family and friends.
Yet because of this time,
I am marked for life.
I will venture from here at the appointed time,
yet because I was here
I could be scarred for life.
Time will tell my story ......

Loneliness

Sitting here in the midst of so many people,
everyone is drinking coffee and talking,
they all seem so happy,
but I realize that I am everything but happy.

They are talking about home and girl friends
and from where I sit there is not one sound.
I want to talk and move around,
but I feel so weighted down and alone.

Like everyone here,
I am far away from those who love me.
This is no time for a tear to come to my eye,
yet here it comes and there it goes down my cheek.

I cannot share this tear with the others,
what would they say, what would they think of me?
So I will take a walk along the perimeter
and think about home and my daughter.

As I watch the rest of the group of men,
all sitting around talking and laughing,
I am aware of another, whose face,
has a sorrowful expression etched in it.

I was right he too is thinking
about the same things that fill my mind,
except in different places
with different people and different names.

Talking to him seems to help me
and allows me to understand that loneliness
is not meant to be unshared,
but it is meant to be done by more than one.

"Tell me about your family,
your wife and mom and dad.
Tell me what you will do,
when all this is no longer in our lives."

I am constantly amazed
that two people can be thrown together,
thousands of miles from home
and can share their feelings and thoughts

He pointed to the others sitting around together,
"Do you think they feel the same way we do?"
We agreed that they probably did
and "Charlie," he was the same.

"Did you see the faces on the new kids today?"
I shook my head and remembered
how they reacted seeing their first dead man,
stretched out and nude in the sun.

"I sure hope that I get out of here alive,"
Nothing more was said about that,
since we both knew that all of us,
wanted to get out of here alive.

There are things to be glad about here,
but so many things could have been different.
I could have chosen another path,
but I am here and that is that.

We are lonely for our families,
we want to hold our children.
Hope is the constant tool that is ours,
along with each other, for survival.

As these thought run through my head,
at speed yet unknown to the aviation industry,
my new friend opened his wallet
and pulled out a picture of his children.

"I want you to have this
because you are my friend
and maybe one day, if God is willing,
we will sit down in a calmer place, with our families.

I held the photo in my hand,
until he dropped off to sleep.
As I watched him sleeping calmly,
I knew that from loneliness I had grown.

Loneliness should never be lived alone,
loneliness should always be shared.
That is not as easy as it might sound
and that is too bad because loneliness is a killer.

I learned a lesson that October night,
about how to live in pain and emotion.
I will always try to find someone, somewhere
with whom to share my feelings.

Sitting here now, some days have past
and I feel better,
because when I was down and lonely,
I reached out and someone took my hand.

So, Tim wherever you might be,
thank you for sharing your loneliness with me.
It helped me make it through
such a lonesome time for both of us.

I often think that I might not have witnessed that emotion,
had I not been in that place, so far from home,
for the war has been many things for me,
above all else it has been a learning experience.

I Need To Get Out Of This Place

The words to that old song keep banging inside of my head
and indeed I do need to get out of this place,
as soon as I can,
but that can happen in only one of two ways.

I can get wounded and in that life changing experience
I will be shipped home
and then spend my time in some bed,
still in a way captive, but home.

I could go home if I were killed,
but if I am dead
it will not matter what happens anyway,
so I guess I will have to stay here,

if I am lucky for about 145 more days ......

It is kind of amazing to think that in any way
staying here could be a lucky thing ......

Take Me Back Please

Take me back please to the sunshine and the trees,
take me back to years gone by, before I die,
to the smiles that are as real as this loneliness
that I feel deep inside of my heart.

Take me back ......

I've seen so much rain, so much pain,
enough to last more than a lifetime.
I walked through so many valleys,
seen so many stars, enough to last a long, long time.
I have done the best that I can in the midst of all of this
and I have had my emotional pockets picked.

I have walked through a thousand small villages,
watched children laugh and cry.
I have had sweet memories changed to bitter remembrances,
I have had my share of learning day after day.

I've sat in the dark and I've talked to it too
and that is all I need of that.
I have bathed in a cold river and a hot stream,
finally in the midst of all of this
I believe I have become a man.
I know that growth has a way of hurting me.

I've been from here to there,
changed the way I look inside and out
and I have changed the way I look at things also.
I will never be the same again.
For months my life has been filled with long cold nights
and I've seen all that I need to see here.
Those sights have filled these eyes and my heart
with tears in abundance.
I have walked alone and talked to myself
time and time again
and I think I understand some things
that I did not before.
Growth and that process has a way of hurting me.

Take me back please ......

It Will Not Leave

This place is all but history for me
for come tomorrow I will go
from this time to another place.
Here is too hard to understand.

All about me is the glory of nature,
the feelings of specialness at night,
the joy of still in that night
and then the morning arrives like a train.

It is so calm just now,
the river down there looks so smooth,
the wind has all but died,
there is peace in abundance here.

Still come that early morning light,
I will go with these men to whatever is out there
and I know well that out there somewhere is hope,
as I know that here it is never spent.

This time right here could be eternity,
but sadly some others we know have already made that journey.
We have to go from here and yet as I think on that time,
I am certain that all of this will never be gone.

One day out there somewhere I will be really leaving this place
and maybe I will see the outside world once again
and in that hour I will know beyond a doubt that
this place and the place we go tomorrow will never be gone,

inside of me ......

Reality

When morning comes crashing into my sleep,
it will hammer on my eyelids
and in that moment
it will end for now another brief dream.

I will wake up thinking of places I could be,
of things which I still have to do
and somewhere in the dimness of my sleepy mind
I will realize that reality is beating on me.

I cannot hide from any of this,
the good choices for this day are very few.
It seems that it is always the same
and that is reality for me in this time.

I will go on into the day ahead of me
and make out of it the very best that I can,
considering the possibilities of which I know
and the reality that reality is beating on me.

My Heart Is Troubled

There is no doubt that as I sit here and contemplate tomorrow,
that in this time of pensiveness
I know beyond any doubt what-so-ever,
that I have a heart filled with troubles.

There is so much going on here
and so much more that can still happen,
that it is chilling to the mind
and brings fear to the soul.

For a person like me, filled with feelings and fightings,
this place causes my world to turn upside down.
There are a lot of questions with no answers
and a great many feelings with no place to go.

These are days that blues singers sing about,
these are days and nights that truly test the spirit
and in that whole approach to life
time matters not, for some have none of it left.

This morning that quality of life
was not very important to many,
for they thought that it would never end
and these hours later they are gone.

Hearts can get heavy here in this mess,
for the things that seemed to be important before,
now have lost their luster
and have been replaced by things once taken for granted.

My heart and my soul are filled with troubles,
for there seems to be no end in sight for this war.
An end will come one day,
but will it have been worth these lives?

My heart and my soul are filled with troubles
because so many people have already been changed,
from young to old
and they will never be the same.

We have paid a great price to be here,
for something that matters to only a few back home
and of course to us who have to survive this time and place
and all of this stuff that fills our hearts with troubles.

A Conquered Conqueror

As he walked away from me, for a moment I watched him
as he sat at the edge of the jungle,
back to everyone else, head down and very still.

I had listened to his story of war,
I heard how he had come here with great hope
of becoming something he would never be, a hero.

As he sat there I imagined that his thoughts were about everything
except being someone that everyone loves.
He had forgotten his dreams and found his nightmares.

When he closed his eyes, he told me that all he could see
were the faces of people he had never known,
dying at the movement of one of his ten fingers.

It was safe for me to assume that he was different
than he had been when he dreamed of parades,
when he thought this whole thing was a game ...

Now his world was different than it was before,
for his life is heading in a direction
that was strange to him and without a chance of a good ending.

He was beaten, not by the hands of the enemy
but by the faces of the enemy,
as they invade his silence night after night.

The days seemed to be alright, as he and others
moved from one place to another,
to find a place to sleep or not to sleep, as the case might be.

Then it happens all over again
when those quiet hours are interrupted with faces
and his dreams are filled with guilt and pain.

There is no one here who can love him
like his mother does, no one who can help
as he tries to survive another night of confusion.

So this conqueror, like a million more
will have to think about these nights for a long time.
Their dreams may be damaged for a long, long time.

For in the midst of blue skies filling his dreams,
there will be a face of someone who also had a mother,
someone who will never see his mother again.

Maybe I should tell him that he is loved
and that he will be loved forever by his mother,
but I fear that will not clean up all of his dreams.

Tomorrow Comes

Today I stood in the midst of such quiet
and the silence caused me to wonder
if a war even exists out there,
I hope far away from here.

There are no tolls here right now
that would cause brother to rise up against brother,
at least none that I can see
or that reach my ears.

All of the pain and transgression
that I witnessed only hours ago
seems to be somewhere else,
except I guess, in the fibers of my memory.

The timeless and never ending
tossing and turning of my mind
is enjoying this bit of peace,
at least for now all seems quiet.

Soon man's disgrace will once again
open its theater of prominence
and he will openly and not so openly,
attack the very life of another face to face.

I believe that all men should live here
in this existence,
but for only one day
and then the very next would be precious.

But because man is like he is,
he has to create illusions
and in this expanse of time, life is joyous for some,
but for most it has been hard and painful,

BUT TOMORROW COMES ......

The Point Man In The Night

I know the story and I can tell it well
about a fierce firefight and a night that turned to hell.
We walked through the elephant grass this hot fateful night,
jungles to our left and rice paddies to our right.

The point man was in his place, the slack man was close behind,
the night had been many things, but so far not unkind.
All at once an A.K. spoke and the slack man fell to his knees
and above all of the maddening sounds, all I could hear were pleas.

I looked for the point man and he too was on the ground,
he turned quickly toward his buddy and crawled to him without a sound.
He quickly placed the man to a point to ride on his chest,
then on his back he pushed, to the safety of the rest.

This soldier then got to his knees and placed his buddy down,
then motioned for a medic and into the night he went without a sound,
as the black of the night was broken by many a flashing gun.
Then as quickly as it started it stopped, we thought "Charlie" was on the run.

Then we heard a screaming sound, and another, loud enough to pierce the ear
and we all knew out there was the point man, and that parented great fear.
He was alone out there in that fight,
as the screams came time and again, we prayed for the light.

As the day broke and we could see, James we could not sight,
as we searched through the woodlands and paddies in the new light.
Then across the road someone heard some moaning cries,
he had found our point man with tears in his eyes.

Though he was not wounded his face was bloody and in a stare
and I could tell by his look he did and did not care.
We helped him to the edge of the road, why was he this way?
Why was his face in such a stare? But he would not say.

Then we saw an awesome sight, someone had really been,
a killer in the night, maybe to him a sin.
Someone had stacked the bodies up and they numbered twenty-five,
not one had been shot, yet not one did survive.

I guess James just saw too much as his buddy hit the sod
and with his cold deadly hands, twenty-five souls he gave to God.
He will return home one day and his folks will never know
how he stole through the night and how his vengeance seemed to grow.

The point man was his job and many others had it too,
but all at once and for sure he knew what he had to do.
So tell your stories of great wars, of hordes of men at fight,
but I can never forget James, the POINT MAN in the night ......

The Bunker Guard

Walking along a road one night in a mean, heavy rain
I came upon a young man who was damp and cold.
I sat down beside him and offered him a bit of food,
he took it with a smile and looked back down the road.

It had been raining for a long, long time
and everything seemed to be soaked,
including the food he had been saving,
until he had time to take, to eat it.

He sat there very quietly and passed several smiles my way
and then I realized that other than me
the only thing that had come his way
was the seemingly endless rain.

Back home if the folks could see him
they would say that he was a tramp
with all of his torn and wet clothes,
he was quite a sight to behold.

I asked if he was tired or weary,
if he needed to go somewhere and get warm for a while.
He thanked me and shook his head no
and said, "I have this bunker to hold."

I got up to walk away and turned back to look at him.
His head was bowed kind of low.
"Can I help you?" I asked,
he shook his no and then kept on talking.

I saw a tear in his eye as he looked away,
"I want to see my family, I want to go home.
I want to be held real close, I don't like being wet and cold.
But I have a job to do, I have this bunker to hold."

I stood there and watched and listened,
he looked like such a mess,
he was alone and very much wanting not to be.
He must have wondered if anyone even remembered that he was there.

I reached out and grabbed him and held him close to me.
"They remember us, don't you worry, you are special to them."
Later when I walked away from him my heart was about to explode
and I remember his tears and smiles and mine.

There are so many here like that, alone, wet and cold,
with thoughts that no one cares about them.
They have little jobs to do and they do them.
They all have their bunkers to hold.

Life Is Better Ahead

They are all huddled around the small fire,
wet and cold, but not so hungry as before.
The day has been hard for the hours have been long
and the walking seemed to never come to an end.

That little fire has helped to take away some of the pain,
but the fire will be out in a few hours
and then there will be nothing to hold on to;
but the memories of times gone by.

All of this might sound a bit far fetched
to someone who has never spent the night
sitting on his helmet with his head covered by a poncho,
just trying to stay dry.

What these men would give to sleep in a soft bed,
to feel the touch of clean sheets
and welcome the feeling of dry clothes
against their wet, cold bodies.

What they would give to have a nice home cooked meal
and to be able to sit at a table and eat it
without having to hold it on their laps,
hoping none of it falls off before it can be eaten.

As I sit here and watch them I am caught up
in the reality that they are not alone.
I too would love to have a warm place to sleep
and good food to fill my belly.

One day all of that could happen,
if we endure this time in our lives
and if we realize that life is far better
than this time in our life has been.

Two Sides

We are sitting here, the great number of the unwashed,
reading about how the untainted are marching
in so many places, against this war and us.

It is so true that we are the unwashed,
for all one has to do is look, see and smell
and even the least intelligent person would learn the facts.

Unwashed in the practical sense, as we are,
there are those at home who cry out about this war
who are claiming to be untainted and they are not.

They have called us everything that they can think of,
they have spit upon us and those like us,
they have made assumptions and they know us not.

We are guilty of being here and they are not,
but they too are guilty of their own transgressions,
they have sentenced us without benefit of trial.

What are they afraid of in this world,
divided by the unwashed and the washed?
Maybe they will find out that we are all alike.

We have the same needs that they have,
we are not all leaders or followers
and we are all frightened at some times in our lives.

We are the unwashed and one day that might change,
for we will be able to jump into a river here
or settle down in a warm tub and be cleansed.

It will be too bad when the untainted find out
that in reality they will never be able to wash away,
that which they believe they are not guilty of.

So we sit here wondering how all of this will be tomorrow
and we will have to deal with the fact that we have been here,
but the untainted will have to deal with the sin of prejudgment.

Searching For Forgiveness

This pain in my chest never seems to go away,
there is no doubt in my mind that it comes from fear.
I never had to think about dying until I came here,
but here that occupies my thinking most of the time.

Watching people dying is not easy for me,
anyone of those lives could have been mine.
Sometimes I feel as if I still have that to look forward to,
as these long days transfer light into darkness.

I am sorry for the things that I have done here
and maybe one day I will be able to live with those deeds done,
but right now when I am not frightened about dying
I am troubled because of the people and families I have hurt.

Those families will never know that someone like me
sits here feeling pain, for the pain I have inflicted.
Some days it seems the thing to do,
all of this searching and destruction.

Then there are other days when all of that grips me
and I can make no sense of any of this.
One day I may have the chance to go home,
I hope I never have to tell these stories to anyone.

I want to hold my wife again and tell her that I love her
and hear her tell me the same.
She will not know the things that I have done
and how I feel about some of them.

I will sit somewhere and think about God.
I want to know why these things happened,
but I know there will be no answers of explanation for me,
for in reality there are no answers which are real and true.

Yet this pain will still be in my heart,
but then the fear will be different for me.
Once I feared dying and thinking about all of that
and now I fear that I will never forget;

the real reasons I have pains in my chest ......

The Agony

It is hard to decide which is worse, a bad disease
or being left here in this place to die,
or to live, if we are fortunate enough
to have any say so in the matter.

The agony of life so often happens to be inside of us
when our hearts and minds seem to close down
in order to regroup
for an assault on whatever is out there.

I guess if the truth were known I have fathered
many a heartache and many a tear
and to admit this to God and anyone who might read this,
is about all I can do right now, so far away from home.

All except to convince myself to think before I hurt someone again
and cause that process to register in my memory.
The agony of life can be so mixed and varied,
but I must remember that others are in the net.

The agony is not this waiting for danger,
it is not whether we live or die,
the agony is not waiting for fear to crystalize
or being here totally alone with all of these people.

The agony of life is not in worries of the mind.
The agony is to have a dream and then in a whisper
see that dream disappear,
as if it mattered only to me that it was there.

The agony of life affects people in different ways.
Listen to someone who has been attacked by his agony
and hear what he has to say about the times in his life
when agony was the main player in that life.

Agony for some will travel thousands of miles
and at a given point it will present itself
at the doorstep of some father or mother.
and their live will be changed forever.

There are bad things in this life, being here and alone
and in this time our agony will present itself to us.
We probably do not recognize the agony as it comes to us
because we are human and not ready to see it for what it is.

We have been granted life and with that comes pain.
We have been given hearts and with them comes aches.
The agony for many is that we come and go each day,
never thinking that the aches and pain of death will visit us.

Then one day we awake to loss and finally understand
just how small we are in the total scope of the world.
Agony is not always a curse,
but the lack of recognition could well be.

Agony for me
is not that life is not good,
but rather that it is and was too short,
for many who have already left us.

To any who might read these words,
many have felt the agony of dying
while others have felt the agony of being left behind
and one day many of them will feel the agony of survival.

In all of this coming and going that is happening
there is a certain amount of closing in that occurs.
Many are dying and in that pain and disappointment
we will close ranks and find a closeness not yet known.

All I can offer up to any who might read these words is the reality that
I have been given two gifts in the midst of these remembrances
and thoughts of agony
and they are both very important to me.

The sheer survival of this place and time,
living through another day here
and above all else I have been granted brotherhood.
What else here could I ask for? ......

Forgiveness

Everyday a special event takes place,
a heart is moved to say, "it's o.k.,"
a baby is born
and I wake up alive.
There are times when we as human beings
find the need and the time
to move into joy,
but also pain and sorrow.
Still I remember love
and I know that it is stronger
than all of the strains placed on my heart
by the strengths here that try my very soul.
Love causes special events to happen,
when forgiveness occurs.
Children at play,
husbands and wives,
brothers and sisters
and those of us sitting here so far from home.
We are all equal to the task
of needing forgiveness
and dealing out forgiveness.
Even in these hours of pain and fear
we can dole out forgiveness
and in so doing we too can feel forgiveness
from God,
which is the pinnacle of all forgiveness.
These events, when they happen,
are special for a great many people
who give and receive.

A Friend

I have been asked by many here,
if I had one wish in all the world,
what would I want more than anything?

"Would you take away all the bad
which happens in the world
and replace it with the goodness you find?"

I have thought about this question time and again.
I believe I would like to have a friend.
Someone who loves me and cares what I do,
someone who knows what is right and wrong for me.
Friends are valuable in so many ways,
especially when the long nights are just that
and loneliness creeps into the heart,
already touched by a distant land
and strange faces every day.
When disaster strikes and cuts us down
there has to be someone to hold our hand,
to wipe our eyes when the tears fall out of control.
That is the place where a friend fits in.

Friends are worth more than riches
and this sounds crazy I am sure,
but only to those who have never had a friend.
That friend cares not what you own,
where you have been and who you have known.
That friend wants you to be safe.
Safe when the arrows of life come at you
filled with all the pain that humanity
can deal a person.
Safe when nature seems to be somewhere
making plans to shoot you down.

I have been blessed for I have such a friend
or maybe two
and in this environment there is comfort,
for here those arrows come with more regularity
than anytime before in my life.

If I had one wish, it would be to have a friend
and if I could be granted a second wish too,
I would wish to be a friend.

Because Of People

I pass from village to village, not able to find a place to be happy
or a place to release all of these memories I have.
As I wander through this small part of the world,
things should not be this bad,
people should not have to live in such a tattered space as this.

All of this because of people, I hope unlike myself,
who are playing a game with lives not their own.
All about me there are frowns and signs of darkness.
This part of the world is in a turmoiling bind.
There seems no way to be able to calm
this churning in my stomach.

I know that one day I will leave this place,
still not knowing the truth about life
or the depth of hope.
Yes, I will leave this mess, one way or the other,
I will leave the pain and though I have had my share,
time will heal most of that,
after this part of life's journey is over.

I may have to search all over the world for peace
and I may never find it, if I have to look to others for the answers.
When my heart is able to release all of it's anger and pain,
then and only then can I truly learn about this thing called peace.
I may have to beg to get this darkness to turn me loose,
when that happens then maybe my breathing will once again be calm.

Maybe one day all of this will be behind me
and I will be able to say farewell
to all the pain and residue that has formed here inside of me
in this strange time in my life.

Still there are a few new feelings being birthed inside of me,
for I can feel them growing,
like new weeds after the spring rain.
I know that once this is over
there will be places, times and above all people,
who will make my days and nights
and my dreams in those nights finally pleasant ......

Thank You, Nurse

She seems so pleasant, that woman in the green fatigues,
maybe that is because
I have been over here for a long time.

She always has such a soft smile to share
and that makes me feel
like someone cares and knows that I am alive.

I hope she knows that
there is someone who had been helped
by her presence and her smile.

Her hands are so soft and gentle
and so warm to my skin
and makes my pain seem less intense.

When she lays down at night to rest,
at the end of this day and others ahead,
I hope she knows the joy she has given to me.

I know she must think about
bodies damaged and broken
and the fires of lives nearly gone out.

I hope that she knows,
that had it not been for her and others like her,
many other's lives would have been burned out.

I pray that she can rest in the thought
that I have been saved for another day,
because she smiled at me and touched me.

Oh Wow

What is going on in this place?
Everywhere that I look there is something happening.
They never told me it was going to be this way.
As a matter of fact they never mentioned this at all.

I am hurting a little bit down in my leg.
But I am alive and that is worth something.
I have never seen so many people in white outfits,
it seems so weird to think about that right now.

I hear a lot of moaning and crying
and there is a rush of people, as if to a fire,
or in this case away from one,
but they go to try and put a fire out, if that makes any sense.

I am not sure just what I am feeling right now,
about being here in this situation.
I wonder what they told my mother,
I am sure she is worried sick.

There goes another wheelchair at Mach one speed.
He seems to feel better than I do.
Maybe one day I will feel that good again,
but right now that is not where I am.

I came over here to this war on a voyage of discovery
and now this has happened to me,
allowing me to rethink that whole process
and now I have to survive another battle.

So, I have to redirect my energy
and see if I can break this trend
that seems to be my charted course
toward a wheelchair and breakneck speed.

Oh wow I just looked out beyond this room,
through the window
and there is life outside of this place
and there is a place where the birds are singing.

I bet it does not smell like medicine out there
and the flowers are not in urinals.
The people out there are wearing clothes,
of colors other than white.

I have awakened to one fact
and that is that there is life
after this place,
for this boy from North Carolina ......

Oh wow ......

Images

They told me this would be a long flight home,
but that does not matter,
because I am going home.

It will be good to see my family,
I have missed them greatly
and I know they have missed me.

That is what love is all about
and that is how it has been for me
and I hope that it will never change.

There have been so many times
when I have thought about them
and their faces
flashed in and out of my mind.

The other images which I see
are only visions of what has been also.
There are faces of the dead and dying,
there are faces of the poor mountain people back there.

I have seen it all on this time travel.
I would like to forget most of it
and think only on what lies ahead for me,
but strangely enough I do not want to totally forget.

Love might be a hard thing to deal with when I get home,
but I did have those feelings before I came here
and what is to stop me from going there again?
Nothing but these past months.

So many things happened this year
that were foreign to my history
and some things touched me and maybe not others.
Those things will affect me the rest of my life.

War brings with it death and destruction
and the death is so obvious
and so is the destruction.
The destruction can be camouflaged sometimes, but not the death.

I guess inside of me those pictures of death exist
and they will be there in the years ahead.
How I feel about many things
will be reflective of this time now nearly passed in my life.

I do want to try to be like I was before,
maybe a bit more caring and human
and aware of the things that can happen
if we practice war and not love.

Maybe the banners have some truth in them after all ......

Getting Away From It

Those days and months in Vietnam I remember all too well.
I recall thinking to myself, "If I get out of here
I will do this or that and fulfill all of my dreams."

Those days are gone, now for many years
and I am still trying to get away from "IT,"
though in reality I never want to forget that time.

For if I do forget that time I will be less than sane
and that would rob me of all the times
I dreamed about while I was there.

I did get away, but I am still trying to this day
to get away totally from that time and place,
which took so much from so many and never said thanks.

I did get away and in the midst of all of that
I was given a chance to survive
and survive I did mentally, and spiritually.

So in this day and the ones which lie ahead,
my getting away from that place will only mean
that even unto this day I must face it head on.

It is true that I could move away from talking about that place
and turn myself away from those who shared the experience as I did
and then find no comfort in helping others find emotional escape.

That would not be a good solution for me,
only an escape to another place which is not real,
a place of uncharted waters.

Getting away form "IT" will only be done
if I endeavor to face the facts of my survival
and they are there for me to see, if I stay and fight the fight.

I shall never get away from "IT"
and that is alright for me because in that company
are a great many friends and a lot of strengths.

I will continue to survive out here all of these years later
because I know that I have other things in my life
and that year served to allow me to cherish the years that followed.

That time was death for so many who still walk around,
that time was life for me because I beat it, almost completely,
that fact alone makes me better these years later,

THAN I WAS ON THE DAY WHEN I WAS GETTING TO "IT."

The Journey

This journey began for many the year
that they headed for their appointment
with that little place called Vietnam.

The journey was to bring change in our lives,
to a point of causing so much pain
that a thousand books could not hold their stories of fluctuation.

There was for the first time, all of the sex we wanted,
for the first time there was no curfew,
except the hours set by the war and the darkness.

The ultimate ability to deal with life
is to have ability to take it away
and that was there with one trip into the jungle.

The journey brought us through loneliness,
it carried us into anger which in these years
still runs rampant as the spring rivers after the snows melts.

The steps have been long ones,
from that place of early purity
to this place, where it seems nothing is sacred.

There was destruction of people unknown to us,
there was destruction of best friends
and there was destruction of moral fiber, mine for one.

The journey has been a long one,
for today all these years later,
it still rolls on and probably always will.

The journey has brought us through anger,
so strong that some in our number
have decided to die rather than proceed.

The journey has brought us grief,
for there are those that we left behind,
friends and foe who died beside us or by our hand.

The journey has brought some of us through guilt,
because of things that our minds and hands
did in those hours out there in that freedom.

The journey has brought us through the valleys of denial,
thinking we are not the same as so many others,
but when the smoke clears, we are all alike.

The journey has brought us memories that will not die,
rather they will remind us time and again
of our sheer humanity and the need for survival.

The journey goes on for many
and that is what should happen,
for to end the journey would be to end life's trek.

The Faces Are The Same

Coming back here is very hard sometimes,
because being here and seeing these faces
causes me a great deal of remembrance,
about that place where I spent part of my life.

It seems that they push me around in the lines
of the grocery stores and markets
and they seem to be everywhere
that I go and where I come from.

There has to be a reason for this feeling
that I am going through,
as I try to face these days
of being home from my first and last war.

Their faces seem to be everywhere,
wherever I go and wherever I find myself,
they seem to be there,
waiting to haunt me.

They look just like those little people
that were in all of those villages,
that I burned to the ground
and stood there and listened as they screamed.

We laughed about it then,
but for some reason it does not seem as funny
as it was when
the sun was as hot as the fire's blaze.

Maybe these people upset me because I am not sure
how I feel about them,
even in this hour,
all of these hours later.

The problem I am sure is mine
and I am trying to understand that,
but still the feelings come,
as do the faces of so many from those villages.

I wish they would just go away
and leave me alone
with just my memories,
but I wish the memories would leave too.

The faces are all the same ......

Reaction

From the thunder that was war has come many a soul ravaged
by the time spent far away in a land known to very few.
Because of the thunder of war the pages of life for many
have stopped turning and the book has been closed.

I sit here in this early morning darkness
and I wonder if any of it made much sense.
It might have to some people,
but now all of that seems different.

Years can change so many things, maybe even all things,
our beliefs, our needs, our hopes
and even our direction
and the attitudes of people who never went there.

But so many went to war
and all of them were different in so many ways
when they finally came home,
dead or alive or both.

As I watch the sun light of this early morning sky,
I know that I have changed.
People ask me, "Why are you not angry about the war?"
They cannot look inside of me, or anyone, if the truth be known.

Why does one person react to war one way
and another still in another way?
Alas, that is how life is, with or without the war.
Nothing is viewed the same by everyone.

And we all react to our wars in different ways
and for different lengths of time.
The only part of the process that is identical
is the reality that we were there.

Mistakes

I was proud when they gave me that first uniform.
I was feeling all of the things that my dad felt,
those things like patriotism and love of country.
I was feeling the path of duty on my chest.

Somehow, one day all of that changed,
when I realized that I was somewhat alone
in this quest to be like my father,
for his world had changed and so had his people.

Never did I think that I would sit these years later
and remember the times that I spent wishing
I had taken another path in my venture
to follow my father.

Oh, I still love this country and I am proud,
but I am not so proud of the way some people
have treated the men and women who went away to a war
that no one intended to win, no one but us who were there.

Yes, there were some of us who felt the desire
to find a way to win a war that was our war.
But there was only our patriotism,
only our love of the uniform present when we came home.

I guess we must have been naive about what was happening,
never knowing if there was a right and wrong,
only setting our goals to be
as our fathers had been before us in their wars.

So coming back home was traumatic,
because our pride was replaced with anger and feelings
of betrayal and humiliation that our America
had turned it's back on us and forgotten us.

Oh, I still love this country,
there is no place I would rather live,
but now these decades later it is obvious
that I was not alone in my pain and anger.

Surely thousands upon thousands have come and gone
since that war was alive and real,
many of them never thought anyone cared about them,
except for their families and that remains the same.

Someone made a mistake in that whole process
and I will never believe that it was only those of us
who were proud to be a part of the nation
that gave us our birthplace and sent many to their deaths.

Who made the mistakes in those years?

I Never Cried Outside

He sat there staring straight ahead,
every now and then he would look at me,
but then quickly he would look toward the window.

"I never cried in Vietnam, at least outside," he said.
"It was not the thing to do there,
but I cried a lot down inside myself."

"You see if you cry, people will think that you are weak
and you will not be a good example for your men
who have fought along side of you.

Oh sure, I felt like crying,
but I did not have the time,
the war you know.

I have cried a lot since I got home, now twenty years,
when I am alone and things are very quiet
and I am feeling really bad about that place.

So many people died over there
and I saw more than my share.
Actually one is more than my share."

Then he stood up and walked away
and as he did the reflection in the mirror
also left ......

because I had left the seat of self confession ......

Those Who Have Lost Children

They are sitting there in their homes just now
and on occasions they will steal a glance
at the picture on the table of a young soldier
who left and never came back to that home again.

Oh, he came back, but he never was
to darken the door of that house again.
At such a young age he was robbed,
as they were, of the rest of his life.

To you who sit there in those nearly dark rooms,
now all of these years later and look at a twenty-five year old picture,
please know we who came back also sit somewhere
and we too wonder why all of that happened.

You have been cut the deepest,
but you need to know for each one
who felt the pains of death ringing in your heart,
some of us ache with you, even to this day.

Many of us came back from that place
and we were different than before,
but we did come back
and that, in most cases was good for someone.

Your sons are never completely out of our minds,
your pain, as great as it is, is ours also
and your loss is our loss
in more than a small way.

Your tears together could fill the ocean,
your pain if it could be measured
would be strong enough to turn the tide
in that ocean that you would have filled.

Rest in the knowledge that someone,
who will never know you, knew your sons
and loved them and cried for them,
when their lives were over.

You are our mothers and we owe you so much
and we will never be able to repay that debt.
Still you would never ask for anything
except one more day with your son ......

Baptism

"Take me to the river and baptize me,"
these words greeted me
in the middle of God only knows where,
but somewhere in the Republic of South Vietnam.

We went that day to the river
and in the name of Jesus Christ,
the words were said and the vows were taken
and lives may have been changed.

Actually only God knows that for sure
and only He is able to say
where those three young men, now older,
are on this very day.

They could be dead, there in country,
they may have made it out of there,
they might have been alright after the war,
only God knows that for sure.

But that is the way that it is in all of life,
in all the places where
we take the time to feel God's presence
and then too God only knows where we are, most of the time.

It is strange that we have no way
of keeping up with those we knew,
but in a way that is how it has to be
or time would not allow us the flexibility

of taking someone to the river for baptism.

The Two Guys

The air in this place smells like old cigars
and the sights that I see are not much better.
People laying around on benches
in search of a place to sleep out of the cold.

This scene is replayed time and time again
throughout this city and this country,
indeed throughout the whole world
and if we care to look for it, it is there.

What makes this time different
is that there are two men talking together,
one an older man and the second is a younger man,
thin and worn beyond his years.

As I listen, they are talking about war.
Their wars to be exact and the times
when they fought their wars
in places not known by many who are near to them.

The older man fought his war in the South Pacific.
He is talking about the nips, the japs.
The other man, younger in his years,
is talking about the gooks from his war.

I watch and wonder where they have been
since they wore those uniforms
and I wondered what they had seen
since they heard the sounds of fighting in their lives.

One was not fascinated by the other,
rather the feelings seem to be
in a tailspin of rivalry
from the point of what their wars meant.

They never knew that I was privy
to that whole episode in their lives,
they only knew that their war
was the worst war ever.

Just two old guys struggling with life
and the results of what war had done to them.
There in the middle of all of that nothing,
they believed in their time.

They were not proud of their wars,
they were not happy that they had served,
they were only struggling
with who had made the most sacrifices.

It was obvious to me
that neither had any idea
that their time of service would in any way
help them through their crisis of the moment.

How sad ......

A Baby Girl For Leo

I look back on those days in the time of my war
and remember so many things that happened,
some of them were good and some of them were sad.

The morning broke quietly there in the jungle
and before long a radio could be heard
and the words from the CP were words that were oh so sweet.

A new child was born to one of our number
and as I approached him with the news he cried
and I just put my arm around him.

"You have a new baby girl back home."
He looked at me and smiled through the tears
and held on to my arm real tightly.

He slowly stopped crying
and turned to look at me and said;
"I never thought I would hear about it out here."

There was a new baby waiting for Leo
and when his time came to go home,
that would be his prize for time served.

That baby girl, now these years later
must be in college or even married,
I know Leo must be proud, if he is alright.

I hope she knows just how proud he was
when he heard about her birth,
I hope she is proud of where he was,

and I hope that he is alright ......

My Memory Of Vietnam

The years have passed too quickly since the war,
some of the days have been good ones,
for the most part I think they have been good.

Someone asked me the other day how I was doing
and all I thought about was the war,
that was so long ago.

Then they asked me what thing about Vietnam
occupies most of my thinking,
when I do think about the war and that time?

I did not answer them,
but I have thought about that a great deal since
and I realize that I do think about the war.

I think about not being there,
I think about how I felt when I left that place
and had my mind geared to come home.

Many might think that I would think about the dying,
but that is not the case at all,
oh, yes, I can still see them laying about there.

I remember their voices and I remember
how I felt when a day without death occurred
and how I seemed to sleep better that night.

I think about the children there
and how they must be either grown by now
or death has found them too, like many of their fathers.

All of that comes into my thinking on occasions,
but I think about the feelings I had
when I knew that I was going home.

It was not that I was frightened by the war,
it was not that death seemed always right around the corner,
it was that I needed not to be there any longer.

So, I guess I think mostly about not being in Vietnam
and then all of the other elements have to take their place
in what is left of my memory of that place.

These Memories Are Mine

Some days I feel kind of sad remembering
how it was to be alone over there.
I have been alone since then
and in that time I have been able to find peace.

Somehow that was different way back then,
when people back here at home
made each young soldier
the cause and penalty of the war.

I still feel angry about how that all happened,
when I think that when I go places now
I am not only excepted for who I am,
but also because of what I was in those days.

So many did not come home alive
and I cannot dwell the rest of my life there,
but those thoughts and faces do cross my mind,
when I am reminded of that place.

They would want each of us, who made it home,
to be the best we could be
and they would want us to be free
of all the baggage that we have, because of the war.

So my memorial to them is to never forget
that they did give their lives,
that I might be here writing down these words,
at least that is the premise.

So the days come and go and so do I
and I will until my time is over,
but I will hold fast to the idea,
that they all died for their country.

I truly do not care how someone else might view this picture,
for everyone has an opinion,
right now I am at peace with this process
and that gives me some truly warm memories.

They came to me from a time that was war,
they came from the deaths of others and from the wounded,
but they all came to me
and they are all mine, all of them

For better or worse they are mine.

Empty Or Full

All of these years have passed me by
and I still remember the times that I lived
in those months of what was my time of war.

Remembering can be a very good thing
when those memories are filled with the joy
that life can bring to us in our glory days.

But remembering can also be very painful
when we recall the times, even unto this day,
that cause us to mourn the loss of friends

We are told that this whole mourning thing
is only a process that time will
cause to happen and then finish.

We are told that these feelings are normal and proper
and they will in some other time,
make us better at the living we try to do.

Be those thoughts good or bad,
there are times when remembering
causes my heart to ache.

So many empty faces,
racked with pain all of the time,
fill so many dreams, now all these years later.

Many of us turned off our feelings
in the middle of the war
and then did things that would change us forever.

But today we cannot do that,
for we have to face each day
and not get lost again, as we did there.

Remembering brings tears and that is supposed to be good,
but inside, in some special places, there is some emptiness
that causes the years to go by less than full.

Years that are empty cannot be full
and yet those that are full of debris are really empty,
the goal then is fill our time with good things.

I think that might not be reality
and yet for some it seems the thing to do.
If I had the key to that I would truly be able to survive.

Remembering And Letting Go

I will always remember those days long ago,
when I was thrown into a situation
where I learned anew about brotherhood.

The color of someone's skin,
the city of their birth
mattered only to those
who were not there in that time and place,
along side of those who kept me,
about my appointed rounds.

Never was I to ever feel that protected,
so supported and needed,
as when I walked along that jungle floor
and slept beneath the star filled sky.

As I remember the times when
all I had to do was wake up
and there I was in the midst of time and place,
when all that was important was tomorrow
and getting there in one piece.

I can easily see and remember some of their faces,
hear their stories over and over again,
and then feel like laughing or crying.

Both, I do when I think about those times,
jokes and then the unpleasant memory of death visits me
and I recall some going home too early.

I remember how I felt watching them,
reading their letters from home
and the tears that filled their eyes
were only reflections of their pain.
They were not old, except in experiences of life and death.
I never liked to put those letters
into their body bags, that was hard.

Still there was a brotherhood there,
there was support there too,
and there was protection for all
from the outside avenging world.

There was too much there to forget
and as painful as the memories are,
they allow me the chance to truly understand
the unique strength of brotherhood, in it's purest form.

The Wall

The day was nearly half gone as I stood there
remembering so many things that had happened,
what seemed to be so many years before.

The air was crisp this December day, but the palms of may hands were wet,
anticipating the fear of memories, of faces and times,
of allowing myself to be lost in the emotion of all three.

I ran my hand along the cold marble slab,
it was interrupted only by the deep etching of the names here and there
and I wondered if anyone who love them had been to that place before me.

As I pushed my hand along the monument,
it was all I could do to hold back the tears
and then that battle too was lost to the moment.

The faces of so many friends flooded my mind's memory,
so many people that I never really knew came rushing to my remembrance
and I was consumed by emotion.

I might have prayed for their release, I truly do not remember,
I probably wanted someone to love and miss them.
I needed to know that someone somewhere wanted to say: "Thank you."

There was a small flag there,
a bouquet of flowers and a note lay at the foot of the slab,
someone remembered that they had gone away.

As I looked around in the midst of my emotional rush,
no one knew that I was any different than they were,
everyone was in the same place, yet a different one.

I sat for a moment on the cold December ground
and remembered those
who breathed their last with me.

It was at that moment that I looked again at the names
and the faces of so many came crashing out of the black stone,
with arms reaching out to touch me.

Their faces were silently screaming as if they had been freed.
"We are glad that you love and remember us, many do,
and we want you to be alright. It's O.K. ......"

I felt as if their arms wrapped around me
and held me so tightly
that I could hardly breathe
and my tears slowly subsided.

I left The Wall that day, but I didn't.
Like so many others, I have friends there, maybe even some new ones,
I know that they are alright
and they want us who were left behind to be the same ......

Alright ......

B.P. On The Tree

The day was very hot and the bugs were in full force
as we walked through the thick brush,
up and down the small mountains and valleys
that make up the Ashau Valley.

As I walked along the crooked little path
I saw a small tree nearly hidden by the leaves,
which had grown back since the visit of the last explorers.
There I saw a sight that brought tears to my eyes and lightness to my heart.

Some G.I. had been there long before me
and not unlike thousands of others,
in bathrooms and on walls all around the world,
he had carved his initials in that little tree.

The only mention in history of his presence there
were the two letters: B.P.
Such a short history and epitome
for a year or less spent there.

Even now, these years later, I think about those letters
and I wonder and have for a long time about young B.P.
I wonder if he got home alright
or like so many others, he died there somewhere, not far from his name.

Once, on a visit to the Vietnam Veterans Memorial,
I remembered that day in the Valley
and how I felt seeing that signature
on such a small tree, deep in the forbidden jungle.

I searched The Wall for names that could have been B.P.'s
and I found three of them.
I will always wonder,
if one of them was the B.P. I found out there on the tree.

I hope not for many reasons,
but mostly because
the signature on that tree
was significant to the rest of my life.

I feel I owe young B.P. something,
after all he did put a smile on my face
and a lightness in my heart and in my step that day
and today he brings a tear to my eye,

thinking he might just be one of those B.P.s on The Wall,
for that is too much recognition,
a simple thank you would have made them all feel better,
if they could have just heard it, but they cannot.

Right Here, Peace?

Sitting here surrounded by the reality of how things are in my life,
I become aware of still another reality, I am far from alone.
The joys of being together in this place are few,
even though it is filled with much of God's beauty
and even though it can be inspiring and filling to the mind.
This place is where sons can come in times like these
and be filled with laughter one minute
and feel the touch of a tear and the stress of fear in the next one.

All of this drives me to surmise
that we are all here because we have been chosen
to hold this place in time.
A honor, I am sure, that many would have just as soon
not been given.
If all of this gets tangled up in the fibers and cobwebs
of one's mind and drives that person into tattered confusion,
be at ease, for life is somewhat confusing,
time is some what scarce,
the body is fragile,
as is the mind.

But the spirit which brings me to this place in my mind
and for the others who are also driven by that same spirit,
that spirit will be here tomorrow
and it will be wherever I am tomorrow and they are.
That companioning of spirit is the place where I live,
because that is the way it is
and the way I need it to be.
That is how it should be, for that place is right
and most often a place of peace,
in the midst of everything including the war,
my memories of that war
and this black marble surface that I am touching just now.

Forgiveness For Everyone?

Trying to remember the bad days is not always easy
when I think about all of the good days I have been granted.
I am one of the fortunate ones probably because
I have had a say in the rules that I live by, since I came home.

There have been a great many days of sunshine
and many a restful night of sleep,
not because I am any different than most,
but because I have had hope of better days.

People ask if I feel different than before the war
and I never let on how stupid a question like that is,
for we all feel different, we are different than before,
because we were there, enough of an explanation.

Still I am the same person,
wearing different clothes,
who I would hope is more mature than before,
but still the fiber of the spirit is the same.

I do know how it feels to understand mortality,
when that was something I only read about before the war
and now when I look back on those times,
I realize that many do not have that privilege.

I view life a great deal differently now
and yet the same when it comes to importance.
When I can see the whole image of this life transposed
on the screen of life, it is good more than it is bad.

I think of forgiveness and it's importance.
It was important before and now that is the same.
My time over there made me realize that forgiveness
is a hard thing to dole out in times like these.

There are a great many people living today,
who for their own reasons,
found a way to show total disregard for a lot of young men's feelings
and today they and we have to deal with that.

What I do to help myself find some healing
is to express to myself just how fortunate I am
to be alive and living here,
with this time to think about all of that.

I have only changed in that I have grown some,
in a way that I am able to deal with those
who would mount an offensive against me.
I like them, deserve to feel love and forgiveness.

Forgiveness all around on me ......

Forgiveness

Years have passed since I was walking through that jungle.
The memories about those days come and go, fading in and out.
The mind reacts to things that are heard and read
and as if in a flash one can be back there once again.

I never thought much about what I was doing in those days,
in the year when my life changed, never to be the same.
There are certain events in that short lifetime
which often come back to me like a freight train running out of control.

I never thought much about dying in those days,
but I thought a great deal about how to survive.
To many that time was only a year of surviving
and doing everything possible to make that happen.

I never worried too much about killing,
because it seemed the thing to do, we were at war.
Knowing that it could not be totally, morally right,
whatever I did, I did with the idea that I would forget it in time.

What does a child know about right and wrong?
What is there beyond the television and the movies?
There is life and there is reality beyond all of those things
and now that reality has a firm grip on me.

I never thought much about forgiveness in those days,
for over there no one figured to need it.
I am no longer a child and my heart is heavy
and I have a need to have someone tell me that I am alright.

I need to know that I can be forgiven
for all those things that I did not consider important,
all of those things that I never thought about,
when I was a child and learning to do some things anew.

Forgiveness, I am told can be found in understanding
the system in which we live and sometimes die.
We have two choices in dealing with these days,
we have to deal with them or let them kill us all over again.

Forgiveness comes when we can truly say we want that to happen.
Until that happens and we understand too, that there is a great deal
of difference between forgiveness and forgetting,
one may happen, the other will probably never happen.

If we seek forgiveness from God, then we have to let him do that,
if on the other had we seek forgiveness from society,
that may never come as long as you cannot forgive yourself
for the damage and horror you feel you bestowed.

The reasoning here is that you in your own way are society,
you have to be able to understand why you were there,
who you were while you were there and above all else,
who you are now, in this totally different world and person.

Quince

I saw him two days ago in the park they call Golden Gate.
I recalled all of the times when he had come to see me,
the times when he was down and out,
the hours that he spent just talking.

I had seen his life go from bad to horrible,
as the drugs and booze killed everything about him
and I listened as he told me about Vietnam
and how that war had ruined his dreams.

"Everything I am today is because of that damn war.
I cannot sleep remembering all of those faces of the dead.
I almost killed my wife after a nightmare."
Then he would disappear for two months.

Then when he returned to see me he looked worse than before
or he would call me up at two o'clock in the morning
to tell me that he had decided to kill himself.
He would hang up then and show up in my office two days later.

Well, his pain, wherever it came from,
was a war that he would never win, we both knew that.
So his life continued from bad to horrible
and each trip into the valley of horrible was more intense than the last.

I watched as Quince lay on that park bench.
He never moved, not even at the sniffing of a friendly dog.
I called to him for the window of my car,
but he never stirred and I got no reply.

When I got to the bench I understood why he had not moved.
He had found a way to beat all of the wars raging in him.
He found a way to beat his abusive needs,
he found a way to beat life and he did,

he just laid down and died and was finally at peace ....

Investment

From that time, in that place to here
has been a long journey for all of us,
but for some the arteries that lead away from the journey
have been more than just painful.

Those arteries could have been roads of numbness,
times of pain which came from being back there again
or they could have been roads where the driver of the soul
had to have complete control or the bus would not run.

Those feelings of numbness and needing to have control,
are both parts of how the owners of those feelings
deals with what has happened to them
and thinking about what is going to happen to them.

Some came back here, those years ago
and found out that it was hard to love someone
like we did that sweet young girl with freckles,
that we courted in high school, all those years ago.

So we get into a relationship and it falters,
who cares, for I have nothing invested in this,
except some money and time
and those things can be replaced.

So, we pack up and off we go, up the road,
holding on to nothing,
for we have few dreams to remember,
but a great many nightmares.

It is not like we had much choice in those early years,
as to how we were going to deal with all of those
who came into our lives
and they left or we sent them away.

The only salvation we might find relating to those feelings
that come hard out of this process,
is to be strong enough to understand
the need we have to have someone in our lives to love.

Then we are confronted with the possibility
of new pain because of loss or rejection
from someone we care for
and we remember the losses from those years ago, over there.

So here we are back at the crossroads,
should we go left or right?
The truth of the matter is
most of the time we have no choice.

We might survive here because we understand good and bad
and the differences between the two.
What is good for me and what is not good for me,
therein lies the soul of my salvation and yours.

Most still stand in the fork of the road,
looking for reasons to say no,
to the love and the touch of someone in purity,
because of fear they may just die alone.

NOTHING INVESTED, NOTHING LOST, WHAT A SHAME ......

Why Do We Have To Fight?

"Why do we have to fight?" someone asked the other day,
and there was no answer forthcoming from my heart or mouth.

One carried a sign that read, "Ban the bomb," another spit on me.
"Get out of Vietnam, " cried a woman and called the war a crime.

You do not have to stand on the earth in Vietnam to know
just what freedom does and does not mean.

I wondered if anyone there that day understood at all
how it feels to be sent to war, leaving all the things you love behind.

Leaving is one thing within itself, but the reasons are another issue.
I went not for freedom, but because I was sent there.

Some of America's children fight in the streets,
they carry protests signs from daylight into the darkness.

Some people in this world are lambs and a few are lions,
some will never work and some work all of the time.

The difference is not where one is birthed
or the number of banks they use in their lifetime.

The difference is that some believe in one system
and some believe in no system, save themselves.

Maybe one day some of those people who spit on me
might realize that I too am family.

I have watched as tears streamed down the cheeks of young men,
so far away from home and feeling betrayed.

Betrayed by the people who live next door to their parents,
betrayed by their country and life also to some degree.

I hope the day will come when someone will take the time
to say thank you for your years away, in a bad time.

The question will always be asked, "Was that war right?"
The only retort that I have is to ask; if any war is right?

A great many mother's sons lay in the cold ground just now,
they never hated anyone and they loved this country.

They never said, "You are bastards for doing what you believe."
The sadness is that they were never given the same consideration.

It comes down to not right or wrong, but rather to understanding
that two people living in the same house can be different.

They can live in that environment and they can have two opinions,
that is what has filled this country with pride since the beginning.

America did send her children to war, at least some of them
and some of those children died there and some came home and died.

I have no answers to why we fought there, except to say that we were sent.
I have no feelings of knowledge as to why we were spat upon.

If there are answers to those questions, let them be silent
for the time has come to change all of these feeling about the war.

I realize that many people never lost sight of who they were and why,
I am happy to be numbered among those and those who did serve this country.

That Will Have To Wait A While

In some ways, I am sure that I still grieve
about the ones I remember who died in the war.
I never knew their names, just their faces,
still there will always be a place inside of me to grieve for them.

I have dealt with guilt, which I never had,
because of being there in that place,
with so many who I will never see again,
for a thousand reasons.

I have dealt with the anger that oozed from me,
as I lived in that time
and as I came home to a country,
very different from the one that I left.

Some may read these words and say that I have not settled
all of the anger that I have about that time
and they could be right,
but I have settled that which will be settled.

Yes, this country changed and with that change
went a desire to forget a whole generation of young men.
Oh, I grieve because of the pain I saw
and that pain still causes me some anger.

I walk each day with people who dispensed that pain
and they are part of my world now,
but they will never be free
of the feelings that caused such pain about that war.

Deal with your anger and your pain,
deal with your feelings about the war in Vietnam.
Oh, yes, I shall, as many others will and have,
but dealing with those who dispensed the after the war pain,

that will have to wait a while, maybe a lifetime.

One will say you should be forgiving and I am,
you should show compassion and I do,
you should understand the workings of other minds
and you should be big enough to set it aside,

that too will have to wait awhile, maybe a lifetime ......

The Question Why

Our lives are filled with the question why
some friend has to die.
To see their face and know their heart,
then we are left and torn apart.

But live we must until that deathful day
when alone or with help, death comes our way.
Try the best to take our turn
and from each experience a lesson learn.

Still the questions come furious and fast,
they seem to linger and to last,
but the answers never seem to arrive
in time for us our life to survive.

Survive the hurt and feelings of loss
that seems to be death's powerful cost,
but survive we just might,
if we never give up the fight.

This might sound a bit strange,
but grasp if you can love's powerful range.
It carries on through all of this world,
day after day its message to unfurl.

You see love even in death can dictate
and from death life can create,
a better place inside of me,
because I know a love has set me free.

You see God loved me enough, even today
to show me just the right way.
The answer to the question why, I have no clue,
except that God and others love me and you.

Someday man may stop asking why,
someone he loves has to die,
whether it was there or here in our homeland,
the life and death of humanity is not in our hand.

So go your way and ask what you might,
but thank God above for life tonight,
because except for a second or a step or two,
life could have been death for me or you.

Our lives are filled with questions why
pain and heartaches cause us to cry,
but never doubt the love inside of you
and go into the world and do what you have to do.

Your answers will come in time someday
in what someone else might have to say.
So listen to your soul deep inside
and from the questions peace abide.

A Place Of Peace

I watched the expression on his face,
it was easy to see that he was afraid,
afraid and lonely, a long way from home.

"I'm alright," he said as I spoke to him
and I watched as his lip quivered,
within a second of a thousand tears.

I hope he knew that it was alright to be frightened,
for to be alone is a frightening experience,
even for those who feel that tears and pain are childish.

Yet, there he sat with no one to be there with him,
but me and his shadow
and a thousand memories of times gone by.

They came from so many places,
each town sent their sons,
to fight that war, I do not know why.

Back then he probably thought
that he would never be frightened again
and now sitting here with nothing, it seems worse.

He, like so many others
is fighting a label that has been placed on him,
and that label just does not seem to fit.

Down the road now from that time,
these days bring back those times to him
and we all remember times and eyes.

Tears have been falling for him for years, I would bet,
because of memories not so sweet these years later,
because once again and still he is frightened and alone.

I wonder where the rest of them are tonight,
those boys who grew into manhood at eighteen years,
who were never lonely or frightened.

My prayer is that they are neither,
that their memories are filled with good thoughts
and that their lives are in a PLACE OF PEACE, finally ......

The War Was Not God's Fault

I sit here remembering those days now long, long ago
when a young man sat somewhere
in the middle of no where, alone and not
and wondered where God was at that moment.

I guess I never felt the need to be close to him before that,
but over there it seemed the thing to do,
a necessary part of the items one needed,
to survive all of the madness surrounding us.

Now the years have passed and the same questions
seem to hammer at me from different places
and I still wonder sometimes where God is,
as this world seems determined to self destruct.

Oh, I questioned the lack of God's presence,
when I saw the result of man's freedom of will
and the total allegiance of man
to everything that was ungodly.

Then I realized and that realization
still rides hard and high in my mind to this day,
God never wanted me to be a captive of his,
he wanted me to be in love with him and his children.

He wants me to love them because I need to understand
just what love can do for us and how it can make us feel
and not because I have to follow some outdated laws
of spirituality and religiosity.

God had no hand in that time and place,
except when his hand was cleaning out
all of the vile that had started to clutter
the very insides of millions like me.

It was not God's fault that the war was raging,
it was not His fault that many, on both sides were dying
and to this day, still in a quieter way
are dying because of their time there.

The whole process was a man made misadventure,
with a few winners and great many losers.
The losers are too numerous to count,
but the few winners, most never where there.

The few winners who went to that war
may not have needed God for their passage through that time,
maybe they survived all alone,
I kind of doubt that to be fact.

Maybe they do not think about those days today,
maybe they never dream dreams about that place,
maybe they are without scars,
maybe they never did call on God for help,

and maybe tomorrow the sun will rise in the west ......

His Miracle

He sat there in front of me and stared into a great many yesterdays.
Tears reddened his eyes and his lips quivered
as he remembered his time in Vietnam.

He never talked about killing or loneliness.
He never mentioned the anger that he shared with thousands
and he never seemed to complain about anything.

His story was about what he called his miracle
and when he related the story to me
his eyes seemed to light up and glow with fulfillment.

He said that one evening in the middle of who knows where,
as he and the others were eating their evening rations,
he became aware of a little girl standing next to him.

Her clothes were torn and she was dirty.
He offered her some of his food and she ate with him,
as the other G.I.s shouted to him about his new girl friend.

When she finished, she stood up and kissed him on the forehead.
Then through all of the dirt that was on her face she smiled at him.
He smiled, looked down and when he looked up she was gone.

That was strange because there was no underbrush near to them,
there was no jungle close to them,
she had just vanished.

That incident was on his mind all the next day.
He could not understand how she could have just disappeared.
He knew she had been there in the flesh.

The next evening as they sat down to eat again,
the little girl appeared again,
this time she was with an older girl.

The three of them ate together and no one made comments.
Likewise after supper, in the wink of an eye,
the two girls were gone, again vanished.

Upon investigation, there were no footprints,
there were no traces of their presence,
but again he knew that they had been there.

Through all of these years,
the thoughts of that time,
have brought a strange relief to him.

In the midst of death and destruction
he felt good because he took the time to be sensitive
and in that very moment he was changed for a lifetime.

It was obvious, as I listened to him,
that it had made a difference in his life,
for all of these years later, those moments still touch him.

He felt good because he had done a good thing
and he knew that in the midst of all of that hell,
a little beauty had come to pass for two or three people.

He calls those two events his miracle,
for that day he became aware that down deep inside
he was a good person and that God had reached out and touched him.

Survival

Fleeting hours still burn in my memory when I recall the days
lost to the present, because they fell victim to the past.
Yet, in the midst of all of this negativity which burns inside of me
visions of yesteryear appear and I am flushed with tears and smiles.

Tomorrow I will rejoice for I have been assured many things
and the greatest of these things is that tomorrow will come.
No matter how man tries to destroy or deface where he lives,
he will never be able to destroy anything totally, but himself.

No one can deliver me into the hands of the enemy
unless I am less than truthful to myself and my desires.
Right now I want to be touched by hands that will deliver me
from this place to another place where peace abides.

There have been times in my life when I have needed comfort as now
and in return for the same, I have been able to comfort.
That is still the situation in this time of distress,
when the whole world seems on fire.

Yet the change in this spirit from the poor and ungiving
to the spirit of children at play flying kites
or dangling their tiny feet
in a river, known to very few, is promising.

The good spirit can bring together the divided,
it can cement together those who have opposed each other for years.
It has carried the weak
on the shoulders of the strong since the beginning of time.

There are endless stories of the power of this spirit,
but the greatest thing that it has done is to change the way
that I look at each morning,
that I have left to live.

I have seen the sun rise and set in a land far from my home,
I have felt the rain beat on my back,
I have felt the pangs of hunger
and the pain of being alone.

All of these things that were once foreign to me
have now become something that time will take care of,
because they are not as important as getting to a place
where those things are only memories.

That time and place will occur
because I have grown significantly
with and in the spirit and that will grant me SURVIVAL.

Our Humanity

I do not always understand these feelings
which seem to throttle my life day after day,
these feelings that cause me to believe
that I might have had something to do with friends dying.

Someone told me that it could be survivor's guilt,
these feeling of wondering just how
I happened to be the one who came home
and a great many others did not.

Here on this porch,
as the sun is fighting to set for this day,
those memories come back to me
and as always they come with such force.

I cannot say that I miss them,
for I never really knew them that well,
but somewhere inside of me
I am surely sorry to this day, that they died.

I do not think that I feel guilty,
I just feel a bit like I would really like
for them to come home, like I did
and have someone put their arms around them.

Many of those who physically survived as I did,
may have never come home to loved ones either
and when I stop and think on that equation,
that may have been the warrior's fault.

The toughest thing about this life,
if we try to understand all of the elements of it,
is that all of the memories that come crashing in
are not the real cause of the pain and the sleepless nights.

The real pain comes from that place in our hearts
which allows us to realize,
that we are only human and we can only take so much
and that is a hard pill to swallow.

It is tough to be human and acknowledge that fact,
for with that comes all of the pain that humanity knows
and in that role we have to act and feel as humans do
and therefore we are introduced to ......

pain, bad dreams and memories and above all to our
HUMANITY.

My Year

I have often wondered why one year in a person's life
can be so important to that person.
It seems that many have felt and known changes in their lives,
since they spent that time in Vietnam.

Many went there and found so many things that were foreign to them,
like freedoms that they had never known
or even understood existed prior to that time in their lives.
It was a time when boys became men, for better or worse.

That time was important because the tides of life
had found a sense of change
and with that tide a great many feelings
seemed to crash into shores of reality.

There was the thrill of being in a place
where war was raging, where life was on the edge,
a place where people were dying
no one in particular, just people.

Then all of that changed when the war was at the door
with all of it's fire and pain,
it was staring right into our eyes
and all we could say was something that today might sound stupid.

That year was important because life took on new meaning for many
and with that new meaning came the reality of death
to those who were young and laughing one minute
and then in the wink of an eye, their laughter ceased.

It was important because no matter what one did
it seemed to be the wrong thing to do,
you followed your patriotic heart
and lost your friends who felt differently about the war.

You killed and then later you felt badly
about the death that your hands caused,
in the name of a war that meant nothing to so many
and a great deal to so few.

That year was important because your life really changed
and because you made it through that year and that time.
That year was important because if you were lucky
you found out who you were inside of yourself.

The importance of that year was in the fact
that in that time boys became men
and that metamorphosis was naturally good for some,
learning to determine the difference, will be good.

That year was good for me, but not the most important of my life.
It was good because I learned I could survive most things
and because I too learned the value of life.
The most important year in my life is this year,

because I have made it this far ......

Different People

I watch them come and go at the place where I work.
I hear them talking about the war,
wearing their tee shirts and fatigues,
denoting their days of war.

They all look just the same and that is what they seek,
at least to these eyes it seems so.
They have found a bond in their quandary
and the world outside will be different because they have.

So many others went there, even me,
we do not all look the same as they do.
Are we different than they are?
So many are still back there in those valleys under fire.

As I watch them day after day,
I wonder how they were before the war.
The war might have served a purpose for them,
it does now or so it would seem.

Many people will be screaming at reading or hearing these words,
for they seem to blaspheme the needs of the warrior,
but that is not the purpose sought here.
Still there is a need to separate the needy from the parasite.

Many surely do suffer the pains of war, even to this day,
but reality forces me to explain,
"that not all who cry at night,
are shedding tears because of the reality of nightmares."

As we try very hard, some of us, to put away our swords
from that time of the unholy war,
we have to all come together to find our strength,
for in that time and place we can survive.

If offense is taken from these meager scribblings
then they must have struck a nerve.
If not then they hold some truth in their balance
and at least one person finds peace in their presentation.

If the war caused needs then, they maybe fixed in that time and memory,
but if life itself caused us to be needy before Vietnam,
then nothing relative to that time of war
will ever cause us to be healed of whatever our needs might be.

As I watch them wondering around here
I cannot but think that they have lost their way,
maybe a way that they never owned.
And still I wonder how some people are one way and others another.

Welcome Home Son

I wonder if there will be a parade for me
when I get off of this plane
and finally get back to all of those things
that I have missed for so long.

Today I overheard some others who were returning also.
talking about what was waiting for them
and they seemed to think
that it would be better to put that off for a while.

That cannot be right in my case,
for I did nothing,
except what I was told to do
and now that too is over for me.

Of course, there will be people there to welcome me,
for I have a chest full of medals,
for all of the wonderful things that I did,
they have to be proud of me.

I will be glad to see Jenny again,
I have waited a long time to hold her
and have her tell me that she missed me,
she is so pretty.

My mother will be there, for I am her oldest son,
my brother will be happy to have me back.
I wish my dad could have lived to see me
in this uniform that he loved so much in "44."

The doors are opening now
and soon the air of my home country will fill my lungs
and those who love me
will hold me close and squeeze me breathless.

There is my mom and my brother.
I do not understand, where is everyone else?
Where is Jenny, the one who would always care?
I know that this is the right place because that is my mother.

So my welcome was not like I planned,
the love of my life had married someone else,
because she did not know if I would come home or not
and she could not invest the time in that pain.

But, I came home and someone did meet me,
there were no parades and in a way that is alright,
for time has taken away from me that old pain.
I did come home alive and that was welcomed information

at least to my mother, my brother, and me ......

The Forgotten Warrior

On the 23rd day of April, this year, on a cold, foggy morning,
I stood behind the VA Medical Center in San Francisco, on a hill
overlooking the entrance to the Golden Gate.

As the fog began to slowly lift, I watched as the hospital ship,
The *Mercy* sailed by. She was coming home from the Persian Gulf and
my thoughts went back to Vietnam and I am sure that for others
who also stood there and watched, they remembered places like;
Korea, Iwo Jima, France, Italy, and so may other places which
related to their time of war.

But the thoughts that rang the loudest to me on that cold, foggy
morning were; "Thank you, Lord,"
because the ship, as she sailed by everyone waving yellow ribbons,
sailed by virtually empty for there were few if any, wounded inside
of her.

Now the troops, many of them have come home. They have had their
parades, their days of glory and their just acceptance home.
Still, I cannot help but remember those who did not get their
true welcomed return. I have thought time and again about this
and I have talked to Vietnam veterans since the end of the war in
the Persian Gulf and without exception, they are happy for the
safe return of our troops and the very few casualties suffered
in that war. They are happy that these American Warriors have
received their due headlines and their uplifting moments.

The thing to remember, if you are a veteran of the Vietnam war
is that the military people returning from the Persian Gulf
got their just rewards largely because you and I did not get ours.
As we try to lay aside our anger and our hurt and we join in the coming
together of our nation behind its troops, for a change,
we should be thankful, that we may be the last Forgotten Warriors.

Through the years the love of our country has gone on without
question, at least in the minds of our military, but the love
for our servicemen and women now has been given a new birth,
a rebirth, if you will. Whether it comes from guilt, pride,
honor, or just caring, let us be thankful that just maybe the
days of the Forgotten Warrior are over.

As Veterans of Vietnam, we should feel, along with our families
and friends, thankful that from our suffering and aloneness,
has come the glory for another generation of America's Warriors.
A learning process may have occurred with some healing ......

Welcome Home

He drove by me in an old pickup truck
and I noticed the bumper sticker that said, "V.N. Vet."

As he entered the parking lot of the supermarket
I followed him
and when he got out of his truck,
I got out of my car.

"When were you there?" I queried.
"In '68 with the Cav," he replied.

"For me '68 too, with the 101st."
He smiled, shook my hand and I continued.

"I just wanted to say that I am glad
that you came home and welcome back, brother."

He looked at me and there were tears in his eyes.
He hung his head and the tears became very evident.
"No one ever welcomed me home, you are the first
to ever say those words to me."

Two grown men stood there near the shores of Lake Tahoe,
embraced and cried about things known only to them.

The Enemy And The Point Man

The afternoon was very hot, but there was a slight breeze blowing.
We had been walking for what seemed to have been forever
when I was stopped by the point man.

As if to wave in a floundering ship, he motioned to me
and as I reached where he was standing
I was taken back by the sight of an enemy soldier.

The point man turned to me and smiled,
he whispered as if we were playing some kind of eery game;
"where should I shoot him?" and he touched his own forehead.

In the flash of a mini second the young enemy soldier lay dead
and then as if he had killed a rabbit,
the point man moved on by the dead man and never looked back.

Now, that was a long time ago and I often wonder
just where the point man is today.
I wonder if he thinks about that day and that shot.

It is so amazing how the human heart
can produce pain or even death and then in the matter of a minute
turn and walk away with a slight smile on their face.

The thoughts that have come to me in this time
can be recalled by thousands like myself,
who watched as life was lived and stopped.

I guess it is easier for me to remember than most,
for I did not just walk by the dead soldier,
I stopped and thought about his family.

I wondered, as I looked at their photographs
and saw the unreadable letters he carried,
about his family and if they would ever know,

just where he died ......

Replacement

People say the war affected me after I got home,
I wondered for so long just what they meant.
To this day I search for reasons to explain
how it was that I was different.

Oh, I came home with part of may body laying
somewhere in the mountains of Vietnam,
but, hey, I am still me,
I laugh and I cry, still the same.

It is true that my marriage
found a way to disappear,
but that was happening
before I made that trip.

A minister told me that
I needed to be observed,
because I was trying to replace
the loss of my leg with music.

I can see why some people,
who depend on the same ministers
to guide their faith,
have their faith shattered.

But all of that was yesterday
and I am in the world now, back here,
doing what I believe I am supposed to do,
to cure some of the pain here.

I guess I am different in some ways,
but in most I am the same.
I still feel the need to pray for guidance
and I still feel the need to be loved.

I still have the need to love others
and to know that I can be of help to them
in the good times and in the bad times,
when the shadows of life get longer.

I have been blessed,
for tonight I am sitting here,
writing these words,
loving someone and having them love me.

Many years have passed since I was there,
they have all affected me in one way or another,
but if the ones that lay ahead are as good as this one,
the trip was worth the wait.

Loving

So many things we have been taught
and so many other things we have learned,
but in these shadow days since the war,
it seems so hard to love again.

Maybe one day that will change,
but right now it seems so hard
to think of being with someone
and then for whatever reason feel them leave.

I never really felt about anyone
like I did some of the guys
that I knew over there
and to remember those faces and times is hard enough.

It is hard sometimes for a man
to talk about loving another man,
but that was then
and these are days when talking is alright, about anything.

My eyes fill up with tears,
as does my heart,
when I think about the young men
who died there in my arms.

It is hard to understand
all of this, if one has not been
in a situation
where they can relate to what I have talked about.

I want to love someone again
and feel good about that relationship,
but I do not want to feel
the fingers of pain wrap around me about them.

I just have to take one person at a time
and learn to love them
and to trust them,
that they will be there when the long night is over.

Return America, I Have

This is America, I heard someone say,
as I strolled through the streets
of our nation's capitol.
So long we have coasted through,
on stories of years and ages past,
but now the time has come
for us to face the truth
about what has happened in these years.

America began in a spirit of hope
and through the years that spirit
has kept our banners high and our hopes
strong in the reality that nothing
can turn this country bad.
But something strange has happened
in these years since "67,"
you have taken away the legacy from some of your children.

You sent so many of these men and women
to a place so far away,
that most had never heard of Hue, Saigon,
and a thousand villages so small
that in the passing of one day
their names run away from my memory,
like the rain ran off of my helmet
in the months of the monsoons.

You cannot bring your children home to shame,
because it is not their fault,
that they were turned from children to men
in a matter of hours and events.
You cannot spit on them
for they went to carry on the tradition,
which was set by other insignificant people,
names like Washington, MacArthur, and a host of others.

Maybe some did not go to that place because of love of country,
but rather that the country called
and in that there is love of country
and a desire to be a part of something we care about.
One day when the smoke all clears
and people look back on those years,
they will rethink who was at fault,
for the war that changed so many lives.

One day I hope those that spat and screamed
will rethink that whole process
and then they will feel
a need to understand what we did and what they did.
By that time others from my war
will have died thinking that no one
really cared if they did or did not die.
America, two sets of your children have been marred.

Changes

People change because time has allowed them to be different
than they were before.
People change because they need to change
in order to survive.
That is what war does the most, it causes change,
a time of change for survival,
then a time of pain for many reasons because of change.

Death is a change for many,
aloneness is a change for most,
fear may not be a change,
but the fear of war is different and therefore a change.

Many went there, some stayed one week, one month or a year or more,
but home was different for most when they got back.

These children of America were no longer children
and to many they were no longer children of America.
They were thought to be different and because of that they were.
So many left the things that might have made them happy,
proud and filled with love,
their families, their friends, their country and their God.

Some say they were angry and history has proven that to be truth,
but they had help in getting to that place of anger and pain.
That was then and the time has come to replace all of that
with something new like understanding and healing.
The time has come for us to once again care about the things that
can make us proud.

From the thunder of war comes a change in the winds of time
to allow us to feel peace all over again.
Those years yesterday and the years which lay ahead
will never allow me to forget that so many young Americans (58,0000+),
never did come home alive.

Their faces will never be forgotten as long as anyone who knew them
is still alive to remember ......

Flashbacks

It seems as if I am back there sometimes
and I am not sure that I am not.
I see all of that crap still coming at me,
in my dreams and in the faces of people I see.

I do not want to forget that I was there,
but I would like to be able to forget
some of the things that still
seem to come at me from all sides.

The doctors at the V.A.
say that I have P.T.S.D.
That means that I have had these problems
for a long time and now they come out, at will.

Of course, it is at their will, the problems I mean,
when they show themselves.
I have nightmares and I sweat in my sleep
and I am often so easy to anger.

The doctors tell me that I am angry about a great many things
and they are right.
They say I need to find a way to handle these outbursts
and they are right.

I wake up in the middle of driving my car
and there in front of me is a V.C.
When I close my eyes and open them again
Charlie is gone.

I see faces of the dead,
I smell flesh burning,
I hear screams in two languages
and I cry without warning.

I watch those innocent little children
running, in total fear,
waiting to be shot at again and again
and then I realize that I am not there anymore.

But there are times when I am there
and those sounds and sights fill up my day.
The doctors are right,
I need help, a lot of help.

The chaplain talked to us the other day.
I cannot imagine how he must feel,
trying to help me and the others here.
I wonder how he felt seeing and now reseeing all of that.

I am here in this place to get help.
I pray that my life can change.
I have no love for anyone and no one loves me, so it seems,
but that could change, I have been told.

I would like to have a beautiful dream ......

Reach Out And Take My Hand

I can remember death and so many sleepless nights,
men who lost arms, legs, lives, and sight.
Crying in the August sun, a dirty face,
wondering why we were in that awful place.

Then I came home to start all over again,
I had lost buddies, my freedom, and my friends.
All I wanted was to be normal and have some fun,
wanted to build a life and raise my only son.

Yes, I did find a place in this hopeless mess,
but I almost lost it all I must confess,
yet, I got up and tried to live another day
and now it's time to walk with another along his way.

Reach out and take my hand, we are children in this land,
pain and hurt I know you bear, you need to know someone cares.
If you know who I am, you will know that I give a damn.
Vietnam made us cry, angry enough for some to die,
but I learned to live again and I want the same for you my friend.
So reach out and take my hand, we are children in this land.

I want to be a part of what is hurting you,
but I can only do what you will let me do.
If I can reach you I must forever try,
before another brother gives up and has to die.

Then down the road in some brighter day
someone like you will turn around and say;
"I want to help you walk in the sun
as someone did for me in 1991."

Vietnam is history now they say,
but I know there are prices you still have to pay.
But I am alive, maybe still not totally at rest,
but of living and dying, living is still the best.

So reach out and take my hand, we are brothers in this land,
pain and hurt I know you bear, you need to know that I care.
If you know who I am, you will know that I give a damn.
Vietnam made us cry, angry enough for some to die,
but I learned to live again and I want the same for you my friend.
So reach out and take my hand, we are brothers in this land.

The Smell Of Change

I can still smell the gunpowder,
which filled my nostrils,
on the day when my life was forever changed.

I can remember being hurled through the air
and the bushes striking me across the face
and coming to rest with only one leg intact.

That was a long time ago,
but the sights and sounds of that afternoon
burn in my memory like the powder burned my leg.

These years have passed quickly by,
but every now and then I recall that afternoon
and flying through the air like a projectile.

That flight is over for the most part
and my life has planed somewhat,
but for a moment that day I though it might be over.

Now sitting here, these years later,
I feel as if I am more fortunate than most,
for I am here, sitting and thinking on these things.

I guess I would not wish some of my history on anyone,
but I want not to trade places with anyone either,
for from the thunder of war in that day

I found sunshine in the healing of self and others ......

Alive And Proud

This morning it was so good to just wake up
and hear the birds singing their songs.
These are the mornings which I thought about
all those years ago, waking up in Vietnam.

They are a reality to me now, not some fantasy.
Laying here thinking on decades of mornings past,
I am feeling thankful to be here on clean sheets
and above all else alive.

Just thinking about forgetting those other mornings
seems to be mentally ludicrous at best,
but rather than forget them
I feel more comfortable remembering them.

They gave this very morning its meaning
and they make sense out of what I will do today.
For wherever I go in these hours ahead,
I will never hide the "68-69" year of my life.

For many who went there and lived to remember those days
are in constant turmoil everyday that they wake up.
I guess because of and for those men and women,
I feel the need to be proud.

Each one of them needs to know that somewhere,
in a far off corner of this planet,
there is someone who will always be proud
that he is numbered in those people known to so many only as

A VIETNAM VET ....

From Thunder To Sunrise

The skies are all cloudy and the sounds of a million thunder bolts
crash in my ears.
As I lay here and remember all of those years ago
when I was in the middle of a war, that was never so named.

From the hours of thunder and more thunder
came the time when that was over
and I was away from that place
and those times that truly claimed men's souls.

Yes, one day in November, I was taken away from all of that
to a safe place, at least from that danger,
to live another day or more.
And now this day, many more later, it is as it should be.

Now when I go to bed at night and think on those days,
those nights and all of that noise,
I fall asleep in the safety of my bed
and in the arms of someone who loves me.

I waited in those months there for the sunrise each day,
thinking the new day would bring safety of sorts,
at least more so than the nights of thunder
were able to give to me and those around me.

Now I greet the sunrise with thankfulness
and with the hope that still another day waits out there
for me to discover new things and new people
and new ways to survive this time and place in my life.

I did live through that experience known as Vietnam,
but others though they lived through it
have never found a way to discover
how great it is to wake to the sunrise.

I hope that those who are trapped still there
in the darkness that was their days of thunder
might be able in this life's cycle
to understand and appreciate the beauty of the sunrise.

Freedom from that place and time is here for us all
and I know that freedom in the sunrise which we seek.
To be bound up in constant turmoil is to live in thunder,
but to walk into a new sunrise is to truly be free ......